TINY GUARDIANS

A handbook on Space Maintainers

DR. UMAMAHESWARI S

DR. VASANTHAKUMARI A

Dedication

To the two hearts who shaped mine

In your strength, I found courage. In your words, wisdom. And in your love, a purpose. Thank you for being my first teachers and lifelong cheerleaders.

Contents

1) INTRODUCTION

2) DEFINITION

3) CLASSIFICATION OF SPACE MAINTAINERS

4) SPACE ANALYSIS

5) IDEAL REQUIREMENTS

6) INDICATIONS AND CONTRAINDICATIONS

7) CONSIDERATIONS FOR SPACE MAINTENANCE

8) CONSEQUENCES OF EARLY PRIMARY TOOTH LOSS

9) TREATMENT PLANNING

10)APPLIANCE SELECTION

11)FIXED SPACE MAINTAINERS

12)BONDED SPACE MAINTAINERS

13)REMOVABLE SPACE MAINTAINERS

14)SPACE REGAINERS

15)RECENT ADVANCES

16)CONCLUSION

17)VISUAL GUIDE

18)REFERENCES

Preface

The journey of preserving children's oral health is as much about prevention as it is about timely intervention. Among the many tools available to pediatric dental professionals, space maintainers play a crucial role in guiding the proper development of the dentition and maintaining arch integrity. *Tiny Guardians: A Handbook on Space Maintainers* has been thoughtfully compiled to serve as a comprehensive, practical, and easy-to-understand guide for dental students, general practitioners, and specialists alike.

This book aims to bridge the gap between theory and clinical practice, offering insights into both traditional and modern approaches to space maintenance. From the fundamental principles and indications to advanced digital fabrication techniques, this handbook highlights the evolving landscape of pediatric dentistry. Particular emphasis has been placed on clinical decision-making, appliance selection, patient management, and the integration of new technologies such as CAD-CAM and 3D printing.

The title *"Tiny Guardians"* symbolizes the essential role space maintainers play in guarding the developing dentition of our youngest patients. They may be small in size, but their impact on long-term oral health is profound.

I sincerely hope this book serves as a valuable resource, sparking curiosity, encouraging best practices, and ultimately contributing to the enhanced care of children's dental health. I extend my deepest gratitude to all those who have inspired, guided, and supported the creation of this work.

Author name: Dr. Umamaheswari S

Date: 15.4.2025

Acknowledgments

First and foremost, I would like to thank the Almighty for answering all my prayers and shaping me into the person I am today.

I take this opportunity to express my heartfelt appreciation to **Dr. A. Vasanthakumari, M.D.S.,** Professor and Head, Department of Pediatric and Preventive Dentistry, Adhiparasakthi Dental College & Hospital, for her unwavering support, valuable guidance, and tireless encouragement throughout my graduate training. Her mentorship has been a cornerstone in my professional development.

I owe my deepest gratitude to my grandparents, **Mr. K. Karuppanan and Mrs. K. Palaniyammal,** and **Mr. Palanisamy and Mrs. Valliyammal,** for their unwavering love, blessings, and constant support throughout my journey and to my parents, **Mr. K. Sakthivel and Mrs. Dhanalakshmi,** for their unconditional love, sacrifices, and emotional support.

I am also truly grateful to my brother, **Mr. S. Saravanan,** my sister-in-law, **Mrs. S. Amutha,** and my adorable nephew, **Master S. Nava Aadithyan,** for being my constant source of strength and inspiration.

I would also like to thank **Dr. K. Ekambareswaran, Dr. M. Ishwarya,** my seniors for their continued guidance, encouragement, and support throughout this journey.

Lastly, to all my friends—past, present, and future—thank you for being my home, my support system, and my constant motivation.

CONTRIBUTORS

Dr. SELVABALAJI A,

Professor,

Pediatric and Preventive Dentistry,

Adhiparasakthi Dental College and Hospital,

Melmaruvathur, TamilNadu, India.

Dr. SHANMUGAAVEL A.K,

Reader,

Pediatric and Preventive Dentistry,

Chettinad Dental College and Hospital,

Chennai, TamilNadu, India.

Dr. RAMESH V,

Reader,

Pediatric and Preventive Dentistry,

Adhiparasakthi Dental College and Hospital,

Melmaruvathur, TamilNadu, India.

Dr. RAMANANDVIGNESH PANDIYAN,

Assistant Professor,

Pediatric and Preventive Dentistry,

Adhiparasakthi Dental College and Hospital,

Melmaruvathur, TamilNadu, India.

Dr. NISHA M,

Assistant Professor,

Pediatric and Preventive Dentistry,

Adhiparasakthi Dental College and Hospital,

Melmaruvathur, TamilNadu, India.

Dr. SHRI MAHALAKSHMI D,

Assistant Professor,

Pediatric and Preventive Dentistry,

Adhiparasakthi Dental College and Hospital,

Melmaruvathur, TamilNadu, India.

Dr. EKAMBARESWARAN K,

Private Practioner,

Pediatric and Preventive Dentistry,

Chennai, TamilNadu, India.

Dr. ISHWARYA M,

Private Practioner,

Pediatric and Preventive Dentistry,

Bangalore, India.

Dr. NANDHINI PRIYA S,

Post Graduate,

Conservative and Endodontics,

Adhiparasakthi Dental College and Hospital,

Melmaruvathur, TamilNadu, India.

Dr. THENDRAL S,

Post Graduate,

Conservative and Endodontics,

Adhiparasakthi Dental College and Hospital,

Melmaruvathur, TamilNadu, India.

Dr. DHIVYA SHANTHI S,

Post Graduate,

Pediatric and Preventive Dentistry,

Adhiparasakthi Dental College and Hospital,

Melmaruvathur, TamilNadu, India.

Dr. SHAILANATHAN R,

Post Graduate,

Pediatric and Preventive Dentistry,

Adhiparasakthi Dental College and Hospital,

Melmaruvathur, TamilNadu, India.

Dr. KEERTHANA V,

Post Graduate,

Pediatric and Preventive Dentistry,

Adhiparasakthi Dental College and Hospital,

Melmaruvathur, TamilNadu, India.

Dr. MADHUMATHY R,

Post Graduate,

Pediatric and Preventive Dentistry,

Adhiparasakthi Dental College and Hospital,

Melmaruvathur, TamilNadu, India.

Dr. MOHANA SRIRAM K.L,

Post Graduate,

Pediatric and Preventive Dentistry,

Adhiparasakthi Dental College and Hospital,

Melmaruvathur, TamilNadu, India.

Dr. ELANCHEZHIYAN P,

Post Graduate,

Pediatric and Preventive Dentistry,

Adhiparasakthi Dental College and Hospital,

Melmaruvathur, TamilNadu, India.

Dr. PREETHI R,

Post Graduate,

Pediatric and Preventive Dentistry,

Adhiparasakthi Dental College and Hospital,

Melmaruvathur, TamilNadu, India.

Dr. RENISHKA R.J

Post Graduate,

Pediatric and Preventive Dentistry,

Adhiparasakthi Dental College and Hospital,

Melmaruvathur, TamilNadu, India.

1. Introduction

Primary teeth are the child's most priceless possessions. They are essential for eating, speaking, and looking good, as well as maintaining the space for permanent teeth in children. Dental issues with primary teeth can be painful and swollen, which can make it difficult for the child to chew or speak properly or even alter how the child looks.[1]

Maintenance of arch length during the primary, mixed and early permanent dentition is of great significance for the normal development of future occlusion. Loss of arch length has been related mainly with migration of teeth following early loss of primary teeth. This has been observed since 18th centuries, when **Fauchard**[2] reported the arch length problem. Later it was reported by **Hunter**[3] in 19th Century and followed by **willet**[4],**Seward**[5],**Davey**[6,] **Maclaughlin**[7] by 20th Century.

Inspite of the best efforts of practicing dentists, there still remains a large percentage of population who never see a dentist except with pain or other extreme condition unfortunately some of these are children, who are not in a position to make a difficult decision to go to dentist by themselves. Often by the time they realized, there is very less chance of saving the involved tooth. This necessitates extraction and the importance of space maintenance.[8]

As parents are the primary caregivers of their children, they should have adequate knowledge about the importance of primary teeth, its health and caring in order to build confidence in their children.[9]

It is also one of the prime duties of the Pediatric dentist to preserve the valuable assets of a child. In conditions when the primary tooth is affected by dental caries it can be managed by their conservative approach or pulp therapy depending on the extent of caries.

Having severe tooth decay, advanced gingival problems, a hereditary condition, or perhaps an injury can cause your child's tooth to require extraction or fall out. In such conditions it is vital to maintain the extracted space by using a space maintainer.

Pediatric orthodontics is an imperative segment of pediatric and preventive dentistry. The orthodontics in mixed dentition majorly spin around the preservation and maintenance of space in the dental arch. Therefore, space management had been given a lot of emphasis in preventive and interceptive orthodontics procedures which includes space maintainers and regainers. Early loss of deciduous teeth especially first and second primary molars, before their affirmative shedding time can lead to varied unwanted consequences.[10]

The primary dentition has an important role in guiding the eruption of the permanent teeth. When the natural process of teeth exfoliation is disrupted it may result in the mesial movement of the dentition, resulting in loss of arch length which may cause malalignment of adult teeth in the form of crowding, impaction,supra-eruption, rotation, ectopic eruption, crossbite, overjet, etc.[1]

Diverse dietary patterns make children more susceptible to dental caries and result in premature loss of primary teeth, thereby necessitating placement of space maintainers.Tooth decay continues to be the main causative factor for the high rate of loss.[9]

Prior to considering space maintenance, a thorough examination must be carried out to determine the patient's oral health status including caries risk and oral hygiene. Space maintainers accumulate plaque therefore patients must be able to maintain good oral hygiene.

This will be especially relevant if the reason for early loss of the primary tooth is because of caries and the child is therefore at high caries risk.[11]

When restorative treatment is not feasible and the primary tooth must be extracted, the practitioner should keep in mind the risk of loss of space and the consequent malocclusion.[9]

Primary teeth are considered to be the best space maintainer under normal physiological conditions.However, in cases with premature loss of primary teeth, the best way to prevent future malocclusion would be to place an effective, affordable, and perdurable space maintainer.[12]

The premature loss of primary teeth is a major factor that can cause malocclusion in the sagittal, transverse, and vertical planes.[13]

Space maintenance can often prevent space loss and either prevent the development of a later malocclusion or reduce its severity. The pattern of space loss depends on many factors including age, stage of development, which teeth have been lost, the presence of crowding or spacing, and occlusal relationships. Careful consideration of many factors is required when deciding whether space maintenance is indicated. Radiographs and space analysis can be helpful as investigative procedure in designing space maintainer.[14]

There are a large number of factors that influence the magnitude of the alterations caused by the premature loss of primary molars, among them dental age, eruption patterns, the amount of bone covering the succedaneous tooth bud, and the type of tooth lost have important role in determining space problems.[15]

The second primary molar is fundamental in the normal eruption and positioning of the first permanent molar. Early loss of this tooth can create a major discrepancy between the space in the arch and dental size .In addition, the reduction of the dental arch length is greater in the mandible than in the maxilla if a primary second molar is lost, rather than the primary first molar.[16]

The incidence of space closure increases with the time that elapses from the moment of extraction. Previous studies have demonstrated that the closing rate of a space is higher for the maxillary arch than the mandible but decreases after the first 6 months.[17]

Space maintainers are applicable dental devices specifically designed to maintain or to create an additional space that was lost due to premature loss of primary teeth.[12]

Premature loss in the maxillary arch may require extractions of the permanent teeth to align the dental arch, whereas premature loss in the mandible may require long-term orthodontic treatment in most cases.[18]

Preservation of the space can eliminate or reduce the need for prolonged orthodontic treatment. For that reason, there are various kinds of space maintainers and the pediatric dentist must decide which one to utilize, on the basis of general and local factors related to the child, as well as the dentist's familiarity and experience with different types of maintainers. One of the important aspects to consider while choosing an appliance for space maintenance previously occupied by a primary second molar is whether the first permanent molar is erupting intraosseous or extra-osseous.[19]

Not all primary teeth with caries require extraction. Although pulp therapy is commonly used to restore teeth with pulp exposure from dental caries, dental extraction is still the preferred method of treatment for extensively decayed teeth in noncompliant or medically compromised patients. It may be the best practice to insert a space maintainer after the extraction of a primary molar to prevent undesirable tooth movement, especially when adequate space exists and all unerupted teeth are at the proper stage of development.[20]

Another common dental concern in the growing child is tooth-size arch-length deficiency (TSALD). Indeed, dental crowding is the most common type of malocclusion. Both genetic and environmental factors are implicated in the development of arch length deficiency, leading to crowding.[11]

The preferable approach for space maintenance is to evaluate the space available whether the space is sufficient for eruption of the succedaneous teeth or regaining space in necessary. Also, true space control involves constant revaluation of the developing dentition. Failure to recognize the deviation from the normal exfoliation and eruption sequence results in unnecessary orthodontic treatment.[21]

More than ever, dental practitioners and dental public health need to know if space maintainers are effective in preventing or reducing the severity of malocclusion following premature loss of primary teeth. Guidelines are needed to assist clinical decision making regarding the appropriate use of space maintaining appliances.

This literature will explain about the pros and cons of premature loss of primary teeth, recommended approaches for space management and choice of space maintainers, and its association with space maintenance.

2.Definition

The term space maintenance was given by **J.C. BRAUER [1941].** He defined space maintenance as the process of maintaining a space in a dental arch previously occupied by a tooth or a group of teeth. Hence a space maintainer is used to maintain the space created by the lost deciduous tooth or teeth till the eruption of their successors.

According to **KEITH.J.RYAN**[22] Space maintenance is the process of maintaining a space in an even arch previously occupied by a tooth or a group of teeth.

The tittle space control was coined by **GAINSFORTH [1955].**[23]

Space control and space maintenance are not necessarily synonymous. The former term, which is preferred, refers to a careful supervision of the developing dentition, it reflects an understanding of the dynamic nature of occlusal development. Space maintaining is utilizing an appliance to preserve space without necessarily awareness of the dynamics of the situation.[21]

J.C.BRAUER[24] defined the term Space maintainer as an appliance designed to retain a given area or space, general in the primary and mixed dentitions.

BOUCHER'S[24] explained,

SPACE MAINTAINER- Is a fixed or removable appliance designed to preserve the space created by the premature loss of tooth.

FIXED SPACE MAINTAINER-Is a space maintainer not indented to be removable by the patient.

REMOVABLE SPACE MAINTAINER-Is a space maintainer designed for easy removal for cleaning and or adjustment.

SPACE REGAINER-Is a fixed or removable appliance capable of moving a displaced permanent tooth into its proper position in the dental arch

According to illustrate Dictionary of dentistry

SPACE MAINTAINER-Is an Orthodontic appliance, fixed or removable used for maintaining the space created by a prematurely lost tooth or the space to be filled by a tooth still to be erupted.

FIXED SPACE MAINTAINER-Is the one soldered to steel crown or Orthodontic band and cannot be removed.

REMOVABLE SPACE MAINTAINER-Is any space maintainer that may be removed by the patient.

SPACE CONTROL

GAINSFORTH in 1955 defined space control as careful supervision of the developing dentition, it reflects an understanding of the dynamic nature of occlusal development.

According to **SHOBHA TANDON** Space management(space control) includes measures that diagnose and prevent/intercept situations, so as to guide the development of dentition and occlusion.[25]

SPACE SUPERVISION

MOYERS [1988] defines, "when the judgment of the dentist determines that the individual patient's occlusion will have a better chance of obtaining optimum development through supervised intervention of the transitional dentition than without clinician directed supervision.

3. Classification of Space Maintainers

According to **HITCHCOCK** [8], space maintainers may be classified in various ways;

1. Removable or fixed or semi fixed.

2. With bands or without bands.

3. Functional or non-functional.

4. Active or passive.

5. Certain combinations of above.

According to **RAYMOND C. THUROW** [58],

1. Removable.

2. Complete arch.

   - *Lingual arch.*

   - *Extra oral anchorage.*

3. Individual tooth.

According to **HINRICHSEN [1962],** [59]

1. Fixed appliances.

   Class-I a.   Nonfunctional types.

   1. *Bar type.*

   2. *Loop type.*

Class-I b. Functional types.

    1. *Pontic type.*

    2. *Lingual arch type.*

Class-II a. Cantilever type.

    1. *Distal shoe*

    2. *Band and loop*

2. Removable appliances

    1. *Acrylic partial dentures.*

    2. *Acrylic complete dentures.*

4. Space analysis

<u>FUNDAMENTALS OF MIXED DENTITION ANALYSIS</u>

Mixed dentition analyses are used to predict the size of unerupted tooth by using the dimensions of tooth present in the mouth. Hence, an assessment about the space needed or deficiency in the arch can be calculated. Most of these mixed dentition analyses utilize the dimensions of mandibular permanent central and lateral incisors as standards. Using the dimensions of mandibular permanent incisors, size of the unerupted canines and premolars can be predicted. Mandibular incisors are generally used as standards because:

1. They erupt into the mouth earlier than maxillary incisors and offer the earliest opportunity of measurement.
2. These teeth are least susceptible for morphologic variations; hence less variable and more reliable than maxillary incisors.[25]

The most commonly used mixed dentition analyses are:

1. Huckaba analysis

2. Moyers mixed dentition analysis

3. Tanaka-Johnson's analysis

HUCKABA ANALYSIS (HUCKABA 1964):

This analysis compensates for radiographic enlargement of tooth image in intraoral periapical radiograph.

Method:

1. Width of primary tooth on IOPA—Y1

2. Width of its underlying successor on IOPA—X 1

3. Width of primary tooth on the cast—Y

4. Width of the unerupted permanent tooth—X

$$\text{The formula is, } X = YX1\,/Y\,1$$

$$\text{The formula is, } X = YX1\,/Y\,1$$

MOYERS MIXED DENTITION ANALYSIS (1971):

This mixed dentition analysis is simple to use. It has the following advantages:

- Minimal systematic error.

- Even beginners can carry out this analysis with equal reliability.

- Less time consuming.

- No special equipment or radiographs are required to perform this analysis.

- This analysis can be completed in the mouth and casts also.

- It can be carried out for both arches.

Basis: High correlation among groups of teeth, thus by measuring one group of teeth, it is possible to make prediction on the size of other groups of teeth with a fair degree of accuracy.

Technique: The combined width of the mandibular permanent central and lateral incisors is measured. This value is used in the probability chart (75% of the value) and a value obtained. This value gives the predicted width of unerupted canine and premolars. Space available is measured with a brass wire extending from the mesial side of first permanent molar on one side, passing through the buccal cusps and incisal edges of teeth to the mesial side of opposite first permanent molar. [25]

The brass wire is straightened and measured with Boley gauge. This gives the space available. The difference between the space available and space needed gives the discrepancy.

TANAKA-JOHNSON'S ANALYSIS: (1974)

This analysis is very useful because it requires no additional radiographs or tables to predict tooth size. The first step in the Tanaka-Johnson analysis is to determine the available arch length. The distance from the mesial of the permanent first molar to the mesial of the contralateral permanent first molar is measured by dividing the arch into several segments. Each segment is measured over the contact points and incisal edges of the teeth. The segments are added together to provide an approximation of the total arch length. The second step in the analysis is measurement of the width of four mandibular incisors. The width of four incisors is added together to determine the amount of room necessary for ideal alignment.[25] The mesiodistal width of the unerupted mandibular canine and the premolars in one quadrant is predicted by adding 10.5 mm to half the width of the four lower incisors.

The final step in the space analysis is to subtract the width of the lower incisors and the two times the calculated premolar and canine width (both sides) from the total arch length approximation. If the result is positive, there is more space available in the arch than is needed for the unerupted teeth. If the result is negative, the unerupted teeth will need more space than is available to erupt in ideal alignment. In the maxillary arch, half the sum of the mandibular incisors is still used, but 11 mm is substituted for 10.5 mm because the unerupted permanent maxillary teeth are slightly larger.[25]

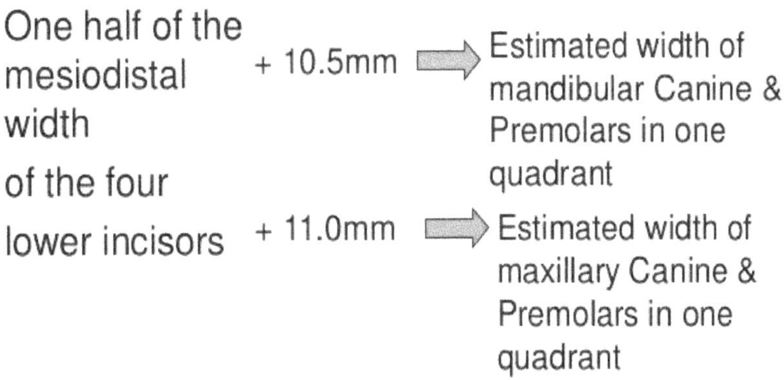

Fig.1: Tanaka Johnson's Prediction Formula

5.Ideal Requirements

a) It should maintain the mesiodistal dimension of the space created by the tooth.

b) It should be functional, if possible, at least to the extent of preventing the over eruption of the opposing tooth or teeth.

c) It should be simple and as strong as possible.

d) It should not interfere with normal occlusal adjustments.

e) It must not endanger the remaining teeth by imposing excessive stresses on them.

f) It should not interfere with the erupting teeth.

g) It should maintain the individual functional movements of the teeth.

h) It should not interfere with the normal vertical eruption of the adjustment teeth.

i) It should provide mesiodistal space opening if required.

j) It should have the simple design permitting easy construction and placement.

k) It should be easily adjustable.

l) Its construction must be such that they do not restrict normal growth and developmental processes.

m) It should not interfere with such functions such as mastication, speech and deglutition.

n) It must be easily cleaned and not serve as traps for food debris etc. which might enhance Dental caries and soft tissue pathology.

o) It should be durable and corrosion resistant.[25]

Anderson and Bonus[60] recommended that the ideal space maintainer afford:

a) Preservation of space

b) Eruption of adjacent, succedaneous and abutment teeth

c) Normal osseous development

d) Restoration of masticatory function

e) Prevention against antagonist elongation

f) Compatibility with soft tissues

g) Effectual hindrance of torquing forces on abutment teeth

h) Economy of construction

i) Resistance to distortion

j) Allowance for adjustments or minor repair

k) Universal appliance

No space maintainer, with the exception of the primary tooth, fulfills all the mentioned requirements. Each appliance should be evaluated and a decision rendered based on individual merit. After insertion ,visual and radiographic monitoring of continuing eruption is advised to ensure clinical success of appliance therapy.[61]

6. Indications and Contraindications

SPACE MAINTAINER

INDICATION

1) If the space after premature loss of deciduous teeth shows signs of closing.

2) If the use of space maintainer will aid in or make the future orthodontic treatment less involved.

3) If the need for treatment of malocclusion at a later date is not indicated.[61]

LITERATURE REVIEW

1. According to **GOULD D.G. [1965]**. One indication for space maintenance is severe deficiency of the dental arch, where it is thought that the extraction of two units would be inadequate, and significant forward movement or rotation of the molars would complicate subsequent appliance therapy.[62]

2. **TULLEY and CAMP HELL [1965]** indicated the situations in which space may be maintained with some advantage which are as follows……

a) Dentition which is not perfect in a patient, but acceptable where early loss occurs in one or both quadrants of the lower arch.

b) In an Angles class II division 2 malocclusion with early loss in the lower dental arch. Here a space may be used to prevent deterioration in incisor relationship with possible deepening of the overbite in the face of lower lip pressure.

c) In Angles class III malocclusion with early loss in the dental arch. The anteroposterior length of the upper arch should be maintained as far as possible.

According to **ENGH O. [1970]**, Space maintainer should be used when the deciduous first molar in the upper jaw is lost and should be used in the lower jaw only when the individual has a tight dental arch combined with deep bite.[63]

According to ALEXANDER S.A. [1987],Space maintenance is necessary when a primary tooth is prematurely lost, adequate space is available and all succedaneous teeth are present.[64]

Even though Space maintenance is said to be not necessary in case of anterior tooth loss, a functional space maintainer or partial denture should be given as the tooth loss may affect speech, induce abnormal tongue habits which may lead to malocclusion. Also, the loss of primary anteriors will cause psychologic trauma in children, girls may particularly suffer from considerable embarrassment.

<u>INDICATION FOR FUNCTIONAL SPACE MAINTAINER</u>

1) When the space for a permanent tooth should be maintained for two years or longer.
2) To avoid supraeruption of a tooth from the opposing arch.
3) To improve the physiology of a child's masticatory system and restore dental health optimally.

Fixed appliance is usually preferred in most situations because they eliminate the factor of patient cooperation and occupy less space in the oral cavity.[63]

INDICATION FOR REMOVABLE APPLIANCES

1) Aesthetics is of importance.

2) Abutment teeth cannot support fixed appliances.

3) Cleft palate to be closed with denture.

4) When unerupted permanent teeth are expected not to erupt within 6 months.

5) The child has reached a mental age of 2 ½ years.[63]

SPACE MAINTENANCE

INDICATION [64]

A. Primary dentition

1) Anterior teeth   - No [used for esthetics only].

2) Cuspid   -No

3) Primary 1st Molar   - Yes [if 6-year molar is unerupted]

4) Primary 2nd molar   - Yes

B. Mixed dentition with sufficient arch length

1) Permanent central incisors -Yes [if lateral incisors have erupted]

2) Permanent lateral incisors   - Yes [if cuspids have erupted]

3) Primary cuspids   -Yes [only to prevent distal shifting of anterior teeth]

4) Primary 1st molars- Yes [only to prevent distal shifting of anterior teeth.]

5) Primary 2nd molar- Yes [to prevent molar from moving mesially and anterior teeth distally].

C. Mixed dentition with insufficient arch length

a. Permanent central incisors-Yes [if lateral incisors have erupted]

b. Permanent lateral incisors-Yes [if cuspids have erupted]

c. Primary cuspids-No.

d. Primary 1st molars- No.

e. Primary 2nd molars- Yes [to prevent molars from moving mesially].[64]

CONTRAINDICATIONS FOR SPACE MAINTAINERS

HINRICHSEN [1962], gives the following cases where space maintainers are not indicated....

1) When there is no bone observed radiographically overlying the erupting permanent tooth, which suggest that the tooth will erupt in a few months.

2) When space available is greater than that required for alignment of permanent teeth.

3) When extraction of tooth units aids Orthodontic treatment and will lead to a more acceptable occlusion.

4) When some or all permanent teeth are absent or structurally deficient.

5) Selected cases of skeletal malocclusion, unless managed properly, may present complications for orthodontic treatment if a space maintainer is not used.[59]

7.Considerations for space maintenance

Before planning for a space maintainer, the following factors have to be evaluated [65]:

1. Time elapsed since tooth loss
2. Dental age of the patient
3. Amount of bone covering the unerupted tooth
4. Eruption of neighboring teeth
5. Delayed or deviant eruption
6. Congenital absence

Time elapsed since tooth loss:

According to **Dean, McDonald and Avery,** maximum space closure occurs in the first 6 months after extraction of the primary tooth. If space closure has already occurred, other alternative options like space regainers to be considered rather than space maintainers. To avoid these situations, the best method is to fabricate the appliance before extraction of primary tooth.

Dental age of the patient:

Chronological age is not important for planning space maintenance. The developing permanent tooth starts its eruptive movement after three-fourth of root development. Hence, the dental age of the patient has to be considered rather than chronological age.

Amount of bone covering the unerupted tooth:

If the bone covering the unerupted premolars is destroyed, predictions based on root development are not accurate. The underlying tooth may erupt irrespective of the root development. It is said that an erupting premolar takes 4–5 months to travel 1 mm of bone

Eruption of neighboring teeth:

Active eruption of first permanent molar can cause severe space loss, if the second primary molar is extracted during the eruption of first permanent molar.

Delayed or deviant eruption:

If the path of the premolar is altered occasionally, it is necessary to extract the primary tooth and a space maintainer is placed.

Congenital absence:

Congenital absence of teeth may alter the eruption path of other teeth.[65]

8.Consequences of Early primary Tooth loss

1. **Early loss of second primary molars**

Preservation of the primary second molar space is key for guiding the eruption of the first permanent molar, otherwise mesial migration, space loss and reduction in arch length is likely to occur. It is particularly important when the leeway space is paramount to resolving any crowding or in order to preserve the centerline. Space maintenance should, at least, be considered following the early loss of a primary second molar to assess its appropriateness, except in the presence of a spaced arch, where it may not be required as space requirements are less or if there is hypodontia of the second premolars

Generally, second primary molar space should be maintained when the first permanent molars are erupted so it can be included in the space maintainer appliance.[66] Bilateral loss of multiple primary teeth or failed fixed unilateral space maintainers would indicate the use of a transpalatal arch ($\pm$ nance button) in the maxilla or lingual arch in the mandible.[67]

These appliances are especially useful when there is bilateral loss of multiple primary teeth. There is a risk of impeded eruption or proclination of the lower labial segment associated with the use of a lower lingual arch and therefore should not be used before eruption of the permanent incisor teeth[68]. Unilateral loss of primary second molars can be space maintained with a number of different methods. The decision of which to use depends largely on the dental health/restorative needs of the abutment teeth.

When the abutment teeth are non-carious or only minimally restored Glass Fiber Reinforced Composite Restoration(GFRCR) or simple wire direct bonded space maintainers are indicated.[41] These can be used when there are teeth either side of the space to bond and should be placed under rubber dam. GFRCR has been shown to have better failure rates than band and loop space maintainers.[69]

If rubber dam cannot be used, GFRCR should be avoided. Simple wire direct bonded (DB) space maintainers have also been shown to be effective in maintaining space in this clinical situation when the abutment tooth is caries free or only minimally restored.[41] Band and loop space maintainers can be used with both permanent and primary dentitions when there is loss of a single molar tooth and a tooth available distally for banding.[69]

However, the first permanent molars can tip mesially resulting in space loss which does not occur as much with palatal and lingual arches as they are fixed to two posterior teeth across the arch. When the first permanent molars are unerupted, it would be advantageous to be able to maintain the second primary molar space in order to guide the path of eruption of the first permanent molar into an ideal position. Literature, graded very low quality, reported on the success and longevity of the distal end shoe which is indicated following the premature loss of a primary molar with an unerupted tooth distal to the primary molar space. These can be made chairside or using prefabricated kits at the time of extraction where crown or band retained. However, this can be a lengthy and technically complex procedure that would require soldering equipment and excellent patient compliance with the treatment.

Compensatory extractions are not usually indicated during loss of a primary second molar so it may be wise to consider use of a simple modification of an occlusal bar to prevent overeruption of opposing dentition if they are to remain unopposed for any length of time, however these are not commonly used.[69]

2. <u>Early loss of first primary molars</u>

Space maintenance is not usually needed in premature loss of a primary first molar if the first permanent molar is erupted and in good occlusion as the resultant space loss and risk of centerline shift is less.[69] For patients that are severely crowded and likely to need premolar extractions, the best management of this localized space loss is to accept the crowding and plan for extraction of the first premolars later. If space loss is of particular concern or a non-extraction plan is indicated, methods described above for extraction of second primary molars can be used. However, where crowding is severe, that is, more than 3.5 mm (half a unit) per quadrants, maintaining the leeway space becomes particularly important.[69] **(Refer Chapter 17, Fig.2: Space loss due to drifting of 1ˢᵗ primary molar).**

One method is to place a stainless-steel crown, with a lab-made soldered band and loop, on a restored primary second molar to maintain the first primary molar space. This is because space loss due to drift may be so severe that the extraction of one premolar may be insufficient to relieve resultant crowding so that subsequent orthodontic treatment is more difficult.[70]

Crown (or band) and loop space maintainers can be used when there is loss of a single molar per quadrant with a carious or restored second molar distal to the edentulous space. Cement loss or cementation is the most common cause of failure in band retained space maintainers. Crown retained space maintainers have been shown to have better longevity than band and loop space maintainers and should ideally be used where possible.[43]

3. **<u>Early loss of primary canines</u>**

In the upper arch space maintenance is not indicated following the loss of deciduous canines, but if there is unilateral loss of a primary canine, balancing extractions are indicated to preserve the centerline.

In the lower arch, unilateral loss of a primary canine should also be balanced with contralateral extraction of a primary canine in order to maintain for center line. Space maintainers are not generally indicated, however, there is a risk of lingual movement of lower incisors and distal movement developing permanent canines resulting in space loss.

Therefore, while space maintenance is not indicated, development and eruption of the primary first molars and permanent canines should be monitored carefully following early loss of primary canines.[70]

4. **<u>Early loss of primary incisors</u>**

Premature loss of primary incisors does not usually require any space maintenance as it has only minimal effects on the developing dentition. Following eruption of the primary canines, early loss of the primary incisors results in minimal space loss.[71]

Space maintenance could be considered if the primary incisors are lost before the eruption of the primary canines in an unspaced primary dentition or deep overbite.[26]

The American Academy of Pediatric Dentistry suggested that a space maintainer could be considered following the premature loss of a primary incisor when the child has an active digit sucking habit, which if intense and for a long enough duration can reduce the space available for the erupting permanent incisor. Counselling to encourage cessation of the habit should also be undertaken.[72]

9. Treatment Planning

Prior to the treatment with space maintainers there are several necessary diagnostic steps...

1) A complete and accurate medical history and examination to evaluate the general and dental health of the patient.

2) A full mouth radiographic survey or panoramic radiograph should be taken to show the presence of supernumerary teeth, congenitally missing teeth, or any pathology that should be treated before the appliance is considered. In addition, a cephalogram and appropriate analysis may be necessary if a skeletal malocclusion is suspected.

3) A good set of diagnostic models are important in the diagnosis of tooth arch length analysis **[MOYERS]**[26]. The result of the analysis will show whether this appliance is indicated for that particular patient or not.[73]

The variables affecting the space maintenance program as discussed before also should be considered when going for space maintenance therapy. As **GRABER** has pointed out, when a deciduous tooth is lost ahead of time, He must ask himself...

1) Has the balance been disturbed.

2) Will nature adapt to this change favorably or unfavorably

3) Is the loss of a tooth, or teeth, likely to stimulate abnormal muscle function or habits.

4) Will the occlusion through the inclined plane action of the opposing teeth, be sufficient to prevent migration into the edentulous area.

5) If a malocclusion is already present, will this have any effect on the space created by the loss of deciduous tooth.

6) How does the loss of a deciduous tooth affect the eruption time of the permanent tooth.

7) If a space maintainer has to be placed, what kind should be placed.[74]

LEIVESLEY 1984 stated that, for assessment of arch length adequacy, the predicted size of the premolars should be obtained and the arch space available for them measured. This space should be reassessed at three-month intervals and if decreasing, then space maintainers, preferably fixed- might be placed.

If a primary tooth, especially posterior one is missing, if there will be more than 6-month delay before the permanent tooth erupt and there is adequate space [either because there is no space loss or space regaining has been completed], then space maintenance is needed. Although this can be done either fixed or removable appliances, Fixed appliance are preferred in most situations because they eliminate the factor of patient cooperation.[75]

PROFIT described the treatment planning as follows[66]

1. <u>Missing primary teeth with adequate space maintenance</u>

If a primary tooth or second molar is missing, if there will be more than 6 months delay before the permanent pre molars erupt and if there is adequate space (either because there has been no space loss or because space regaining has been completed) then space maintenance is needed. Although this can be done with either fixed or removable appliances. Fixed appliances are preferred in most situations because they eliminate the factor of patient cooperation. If the space is unilateral, it can be managed by unilateral fixed appliance.

If molars on both sides have been lost and the lateral incisors have erupted, it is usually better to place a lingual arch rather than 2 unilateral appliances early loss of a single primary canine in the mixed dentition requires space maintenance or extraction of the contra lateral tooth to eliminate mid line changes and the development of arch symmetry. If the contra lateral canine is extracted, a lingual; arch space maintainer may still be needed to prevent lingual movement of the incisors.

2. <u>Localized space loss [3mm or less] Space regaining</u>

Potential space problems can be created by drift of permanent incisors or molars, after premature extraction of primary canines or molars. In children who meet the criteria for moderate problems.i.e., no skeletal involvement, lost space can be regained by repositioning the teeth that have drifted then a space maintainer is necessary to prevent the further drift and space loss until the succedaneous teeth have erupted. A space maintainer alone is not adequate treatment for a space deficiency.

Depending   upon the space analysis the line of treatment and its prognosis in the space management of mixed dentition was well discussed by **LOUIS A et al[1975].**[76]

They said determination of the nature and the timing of treatment during the period of the mixed dentition can involve complex diagnostic problems. Evaluation of patients' profile is important in determining his facial growth pattern. Errors in the sequence of tooth eruption and aberration in development should be expected to complicate space management. Space analysis is based on assumptions that no inharmonious growth patterns are present, that there will be minimal jaw growth in the area of tooth eruption and that correctly related jaws will continue to grow normally.

Usually, appliances designed to regain space are not very complex and prognosis is good. The timing of treatment is related to whether the space loss is static or progressive. Early regaining of space poses the problem of maintaining the position of the developing 2nd permanent molar.

To create space in the sagittal dimension, treatment is begun to conjunction with the exfoliation of primary posterior teeth whether the treatment is begun to create space in the transverse dimension depends on the degree of of skeletal involvement and whether or not a functional occlusion exists. If a space discrepancy exceeds 5 mm and is superimposed on severe crowding or protrusion, it is usually necessary to extract permanent teeth to achieve a good occlusion. [76]

10. Appliance Selection

There are some factors that govern the selection of space maintaining appliance. We have to consider those factors before naming the special appliance, fixed or removable. Often two types of appliances may be used to accomplish the task.[21]

1. **Patient cooperation**

Greater patient cooperation is needed for removable appliances. Unlike fixed appliance patients, removable appliance wearers should wear the appliance for the given time. Most dentists experience the situation wherein patient arrives with his appliance in hand which was taken out sometimes ago. By this time some space has been lost and reassessment of space is needed. Often space maintainer may be replaced by regaining appliance, thus cooperation of the patient is a key factor governing the selection of the appliance.

2. **Integrity of the appliance**

When considering long term wear, the frequency with which the appliances break or are lost, must be considered. All types of appliances suffer breakage. Careful examination of appliances often reveals inherent flaws in their construction. Failure to encase a wire in solder, remnants of flux and wires thinned by polishing are some of the technical problems frequently seen. Mandibular removable appliances will have a higher incidence of fracture than other types of appliances. Generally, appliance integrity is greater with fixed appliances.

3. <u>Maintenance</u>

With normal usage, the clasp, the acrylic or removable appliance may require minor adjustments. The cement on the abutment areas of the fixed appliances often disintegrates with time and loose bands will lead to decalcification of the underlying enamel due to the food stagnation and acid production. Thus, periodic removal of appliance, checking for decalcification, polishing of the tooth and cementation is necessary for fixed appliances. The length of time an appliance is required and the projected maintenance should be considered when making the selection of appliance.

4. <u>Modifiability</u>

If a successor tooth erupts out of alignment, the wire of a fixed appliance may be difficult to adjust. On the other hand, if a removable appliance has been used, trimming of acrylic might allow for the malalignment. The dynamic individual situations must be considered. Anticipating future modifications owing to occlusal development can reduce the number of appliances required and influence the selection of appliance.

5. <u>Limitations</u>

A band and loop appliance at age seven may suffice for controlling the space created by extraction of a 2nd primary molar. However, if the eruption sequence follows a normal pattern, the 1st primary molar abutment will be shed before the appliance has served its purpose. Consequently, the band-loop appliance has time limitations and may have to be replaced. The clinician should project the number of appliances needed for the patient whenever possible.

6. <u>Cost</u>

Usually, the time required to construct removable acrylic appliances is greater than for fixed non-acrylic appliances. Its labor cost rise, the increasing economic implication of treatment will dictate the nature of treatment to some extent. For this reason, efficient directly bonded appliances, which do not require laboratory services, offer a fertile area for future clinical research.[21]

11. Fixed Space Maintainers

1. **BAND CONSTRUCTION**

The making of a properly fitting contoured, strong band is a very important undertaking for fixed appliances or space maintainers .[28]

Bands can be prepared by pinching from roles of band material or preformed seamless bands can be used.

a) Band material

Band material comes in two different widths and in thickness. Usually, for 1st molars, 0.006-inch stainless steel band material is used. On the 2nd deciduous molars, the diameter of the completed band is such that 0.005-inch-thick material is sufficient.

b) Tooth separation

If the space present mesial and distal to the tooth to be banded is not sufficient for the band, the space is created by tooth separation. Separation may be done by brass separating wires or rubber wedges. If young adults or children the brass wire is kept for 4 or 5 days. The separation probably occurs earlier than 4 or 5 days in many people. But it is stated that the separating wires should not be kept for more than a week.

c) Molar band separation

The molar band will be made from 0.006 x 0.180-inch stainless steel band material. This has a dull side and a shiny side the dull side goes next to the tooth and the shiny side faces outwards. The dullness helps to hold the cement in place, and the shiny side lets foods slide off.

About 2.75 inch of band material is cut off with straight scissors and a loop is made with the two dull sides against each other. This has to be spot welded. It will be helpful to dip the end in a mixture of alcohol and water. This does two things, it helps to clean the band, making a better contact.
It also dissipates some heat and the visible vapor is evidence that a joined has been made. The tangent ends of the band material are rounded with curved crown and bridge scissors, so as not to cut into patients check.

The band material then slipped down the tooth structure and trial pinching are made with band forming pliers. Sometimes trial pinch will be made with the hoe pliers. If hoe pliers are used, prior contouring should be done with contouring pliers.

d) Differences in pinching the upper and lower bands [28]

The upper band is usually pulled from the palatal side, where as the lower molar band is pulled from buccal side.
The seam of the upper band will be kept at the mesiolingual line angle whereas for lower at the mesiobuccal line angle.
This will place the seam opposite the 5th cusp in the upper whereas for lower band it will be opposite the mesiobuccal cusp.
It is better to have the seam opposite a cusp than a groove. It is more difficult to adapt two thickness of band material [the seam plus the patch] into a groove.

If the placed in proper position the occlusal surface of the band should be parallel to the occlusal surface of the tooth. Mesially and distally the occlusal surface of the band should be just below the crest of the mesial marginal ridge and just above the mesial crest of curvature [represented by the contact area].

The band carried by hoe pliers, is placed down the tooth by using the thumb, as far as it will comfortably go, keeping the tails of the band in the hoe pliers at the mesiobuccal line angle in case of lower and mesiolingual line angle in case of upper bands.

Holding the band in place, we have to squeeze the hoe pliers up against the crease formed by the two tails of the band material. The band is removed by gently wiggling it occlusally by means of the two tails. Either fingers or pliers are used for this purpose.

Now the new, closer seam is spot welded with three or four spot welds. At this point festooning and contouring may be required. Festooning is done with a curved crown-and bridge scissors. For lower 1st molar because of the rhombus shape of the tooth [mesially and distally] the band needs to be trimmed or festooned at the lingual cervical area. Buccal festooning will be done later because tails at the seam have to be removed.

For upper band festooning and trimming of the cervical area lingually or buccal occlusal portion usually is not necessary.

Cresent shaped pieces of band material are removed from the cervical area mesially and distally. These concave cuts are blended into the buccal and lingual cervical portions of the band by a file or grinding wheel and an abrasive rubber wheel. Then the band is cleansed with a cotton roll dipped into alcohol water mixture.

We can use the special tongue and groove pliers [band forming pliers] for the second pull up of the band. It automatically puts contour into the band as the final squeeze takes place.

Then the band is further seated on to the tooth, Because of the initial pull up of the hoe pliers and the closer spot welds, the band may not yet be all the way down to its correct position.[28]

Now a band adaptor or band pusher is taken and press down mesially, distally, and buccally. The lower band is almost never pushed from lingual, as this would roll the band to far cervically on the lingual surface. Like-wise from buccal in case of upper band.

Again, band forming pliers and/ or hoe pliers is used to final adaptation of the band, and the band is removed from the tooth. This is done by using band removing pliers. At this point we may find the band rolling cervically on lingual side of lower or buccal side of upper bands. A hook sealer may be used to slip it far enough from cervically during removal of the band.

Once the band is removed from the mouth, the saliva [and blood] is washed off. The band is dipped in alcohol-water mixture and spot welded along the curved seam. The seam is curved because of the contour of the ends of the pliers. The excess band material along the marginal ridges is cut off and smoothened.

e) Extensions of the band

The mesial and distal occlusal surfaces will be just below the crest of the marginal ridges, but above the contact area.

Lingually the occlusal surface will be just below the depth of the lingual developmental groove. Buccally the band will be far enough down on the buccal surface to avoid occlusal interference.

In order to prevent food stagnation, the band should either extend below the gingival margin or at the edge of the band should be cut well away from the gingival margin to permit self-cleansing of the cervical portion of the tooth.

After final adaptation of the band the tag is adapted closely to the buccal surface of lower band and to the palatal of the upper band. The band is removed from the tooth and the adapted tag portion is welded to the band after dipping into alcohol-water mixture.

Then a wheel stone is used to grind the seam flat. An abrasive rubber wheel is used to smooth the surface and edges of the seam.

The band is again seated onto the tooth. Now the band adaptor / amalgam condenser is taken and the band material is adapted into the buccal and lingual developmental grooves from occlusal to cervical margins. Any free-standing band material on the distal is pulled towards the marginal ridge. The band adaptor is used all around the occlusal surface, pushing the band material in towards the tooth where any gaps show up.

The band is now complete and should be removed for adding of attachments, either by spot welding or soldering. [28]

2. IMPRESSION TAKING AND CAST PREPARATION

An alginate or compound impression of the banded teeth and appropriate abutment is made. Full arch impressions are taken for Lingual arch and Nance appliance fabrication. A sectional impression utilizing a universal swivel tray is adequate when planning a band and loop or crown-loop space maintainer.

After taking the impression band remover pliers are used to remove the band. A cotton roll should be placed on the occlusal surface of the tooth unless the tip of the band remover has a rubber or soft plastic covering. the soft covering [or optional cotton roll] prevents cuspal fracture.

The band is placed into the impression in position it occupied on the tooth and secured for stability during cast pouring. The prepared impression is poured in stone to form the working case.[28]

3. LOOP / ARCH CONSTRUCTION

The loop is fashioned from a standard 0.036 wire with no.120 and no.139 pliers and wire cutter. LOOS P.J and CORPRON R.E. [1972] discussed about the factors that should be incorporated in the design of the wire loop. The design of the loop for each appliance is unique and discussed under each appliance separately.[77]

4. SOLDERING

Asbestos putty or quick set plaster is used to position the adapted wire on the working model, the model is placed on the soldering block. A blow pipe flame of approximately 1 ½ inches or solder torch is used for soldering. All soldering should be done 3 mm beyond the blue cone in the reducing zone of the flame. The joint formed by the wire and band should never exceed a dull red collar during the soldering process. A thin needle-like flame will prevent over heating of the metal surrounding the solder joint.

A generous amount of borax type flux should be applied to the solder join .The flux must be applied above and below the point where wire contacts band . A piece of solder 3-4 mm in length is cut and the flame directed towards the solder joint. As the flux melts, a piece of solder is transferred to the solder joint with a pair of utility pliers.

The flame is redirected toward the solder and this position is maintained until the solder has flowed. The solder must flow smoothly over the wire to form a solid union between the band and the wire. This procedure is repeated to the opposite side. The hardness of the stone has been destroyed by the heating process, and the appliance may be easily removed from the working model. The stone adhering to the center of the band is removed and the appliance is rinsed by water.[77]

5. <u>POLISHING</u>

A four-step procedure is used to polish the stainless-steel appliances. A finished solder joint should be smooth transition with the band. Rubber wheels are relied upon to reduce surface roughness. Final polish is accomplished with gold rouge on rag wheel. The acrylic button of the Nance appliance is trimmed and smoothed with an acrylic bur and then polished with pumice.[28]

FIXED SPACE MAINTAINERS

Fixed space maintainers are the appliance utilizing bands or crowns for their construction. Common fixed space maintainers include...

1) Band and loop.

2) Crown and loop.

3) Lingual arch.

4) Palatal arches, which includes,

5) Nance palatal holding arch.

6) Transpalatal arch.

7) Distal shoe space maintainer.

8) Fixed appliances for anterior space maintenance.

9) Various other fixed appliances are also discussed.

BAND AND LOOP SPACE MAINTAINER

Band and loop space maintainer is one of the commonest space controlling appliances used in the dental practice. It is a unilateral fixed appliance indicated for space maintenance in the posterior segments when single tooth is lost.

Indication

It is usually indicated for preserving the space created by the premature loss of single primary molar.

a. A favorite application is controlling space created by the early loss of primary molar in the primary dentition.

b. Bilateral loss of single primary molar before eruption of the permanent incisors.

c. It is also indicated when second primary molar is lost after the eruption of first permanent molar.

d. Sometimes it is given in cases of premature loss of primary canines.

Usually Band and loop space maintainer is not indicated to preserve the space created by two adjacent primary molars. The lengthy loop created in these situations is more susceptible to the forces of mastication, thus the appliance is less stable.[21]

Advantages

1. It is an effective space maintainer for unilateral loss of single tooth in buccal   segments.
2. It is economical to make and construction is simple.
3. It makes little chair time, if preformed bands are used.
4. It adjusts easily to accommodate the changing dentition.

<u>**Disadvantages**</u>

1. Like any other fixed maintainers, decalcification under the band is a problem.
2. It will not prevent the continued eruption of the opposing teeth.
3. It does not restore the chewing function.
4. Limited to maintenance of a single tooth space.

<u>**Construction of the appliance**</u>

Usually, band is fitted or adapted to the tooth posterior to the edentulous area or site of premature loss of tooth. Sometimes 1st deciduous molar is preferred for banding when 2nd deciduous molar is lost instead of 1st permanent molar because of decalcification problem underneath the bands. But the disadvantage here is exfoliation of abutment or banded tooth before the purpose is served [before the eruption of 2nd premolar.]

Occasionally the tooth anterior to the missing tooth may have a distal undercut which can interfere with the path of insertion of the space maintainer. This happens more often in the lower arch. The distal undercut should be removed with a fine diamond bur, so that the loop of the space maintainer can butt against the distal surface of the tooth.

After adaptation of the band, a full length of alginate impression or a low fussing compound impression is taken .The impression should include the banded tooth, edentulous space, and the tooth mesial to the space .The band is removed from the tooth and positioned in the impression and seated with sticky wax .The impression then poured in stone and cast is made.[79]

Design of the wire loop

The loop is fashioned from a standard 0.036 wire with no.120 and no.139 pliers and wire cutter.

LOOS P.J and CORPRON R.E. [1972] discussed about the factors that should be incorporated in the design of the wire loop.

The mesial end of the loop should start distally from lingual to buccal. This design allows the increase in inter canine without any obstruction.

The final width of the loop should be wide enough to allow eruption of the premolar inside the loop.

The distal ends of the loop should overlap the mesial one third of the buccal and lingual surfaces of the band, just above the free gingival margin, to allow occlusal clearance adequate strength of the soldered joints in these areas. The arms should run on each side of the alveolar ridge close to or resting gently on the gingival but not impinging onto the gingiva.[77]

Soldering the loop to the band

By securing the anterior part of the loop in position to the model with sticky wax, the wax is then covered with plaster. Flux is applied to the wire bands and underlying band and is heated with the soldering flame until it flows around the wire. The surface of the band and the wire must be clean for satisfactory soldering.

Finishing the appliance

The appliance is removed from the model. If the band was trimmed gingivally, the margin should be tapered to a knife edge with a sand paper disk. The appliance is polished with fine pumice and a stainless-steel wire wheel. The appliance will be ready for cementation. **(Refer Chapter 17. Fig.3: Band and Loop space maintainer).**

CROWN AND LOOP SPACE MAINTAINER

Crown and loop appliance will be similar to band and loop space maintainer in all respects except that stainless steel crown is used for the abutment tooth. [22]

Indication

Most of the indications of the band –loop appliance also applied to the crown –loop. The crown is used in preference to the band when the abutment tooth is;

1. Highly carious.
2. Exhibits marked Hypoplasia.
3. Pulpotomies.

Technique

The technique for use of the crown-loop is similar to that of band-loop appliance. A stainless-steel crown is fitted to the abutment tooth, an impression is taken, and so forth. It is usually necessary between the preparatory appointment to place a temporary crown on the abutment tooth. The temporary crown serves two main purposes; It eliminates sensitivity and it prevents closure of space between the prepared tooth and an adjacent tooth while the appliance is being fabricated.[22]

Another approach to the crown and loop appliance is to place a band-loop appliance over the crown. In this manner, the need for a temporary crown is eliminated. If difficulty is experienced when fitting band over the crown, the next the next largest size can use.

The loop is directly soldered to the crown directly to the crown directly or to the band is adapted over the crown.

Stainless steel crowns in construction of space maintainers

Stainless steel crowns in the construction of space maintainers were discussed by PRUHS R.J. IN (1978).

Preformed stainless-steel crowns can be advantageously used in the design and construction of space maintainers. They offer several benefits over bands: decalcification and recurrent caries are less likely because the clinical crown is completely covered, retention is improved, and the crowns do not need to be removed and recemented during the course of treatment.

When used on primary molars, stainless steel crowns require tooth preparation. When they are used in permanent teeth for the construction of a lingual arch, however, the abutment teeth should not be prepared. The bite will be slightly open at first, but it will soon close.

When stainless steel crowns are used in the construction of lingual arch, it is important to inform the child's parents that the teeth beneath the crowns are healthy and that the crown will be removed when space maintenance is no longer necessary.[22] **(Refer Chapter 17. Fig.3: Crown and Loop space maintainer).**

THE LINGUAL ARCH SPACE MAINTAINER

The Lingual arch is the most effective appliance for space maintenance and minor tooth movement in the lower arch. The classical mandibular arch wire consists of two bands cemented to the first permanent molars or sometimes second deciduous molars, which are joined by a stain less steel wire butting against four incisors.

Indication

The appliance is usually indicated to preserve the spaces created by the multiple loss of primary molars when there is no loss of space in the arch and a favorable mixed dentition analysis.

The use of a lingual arch is a good preventive measure, since it helps in maintaining the arch perimeter by preventing both mesial drifting and lingual of the molar teeth and also lingual collapse of the anterior teeth.

Numerous modifications of the appliance have been used. Spurs i.e., projections of wire, may be used as stoppers distal to anterior teeth to prevent their tipping or migration distally in the arch. These helps in maintaining symmetry of center lines, especially in cases of unilateral tooth loss.[73]

Advantages

1. It is an excellent source of anchorage, because it incorporates resistance of several teeth.
2. It allows free individual movements of teeth while maintaining.
3. It causes little or no inconvenience to the patient.
4. It is less bulky than removable acrylic space maintainer.
5. It is less conspicuous than outer space maintainers.
6. It serves as a space maintainer for more than one succedaneous tooth in the arch.

Disadvantages

1. As with other fixed appliances, prolonged use of orthodontic

2. bands on a tooth may facilitate the decalcification of the tooth. Thus, whenever possible it is better to prefer 2nd primary molar for banding.

3. The arch wire may become embedded into the soft tissue. This seems to occur more often in patients with poor oral hygiene.

4. The wire may be distorted by masticatory forces and move teeth into undesirable positions. It is there for necessary to have the patient return often to the dental office for cheek ups. The appliance should be removed every year and inspected for damage and further usefulness, and then recemented onto teeth that have had a topical fluoride treatment.

Tsamtsouris and George [1977] discussed a case involving lingual arch appliance with bilateral loss of deciduous molars.73

Fabrication of the appliance

First Clinical procedure

This phase consists of construction of molar bands for the two molars to be banded, impression taking and transfer of bands onto the models.[21]

Laboratory procedure

Mandibular arch wires are usually 0.036 to 0.040 inch in diameter. Smaller diameter wires are not used they may not withstand the forces of mastication.

Arch design

Arch design should be directed toward minimizing the maintenance problems. The arch wire should contact the erupted permanent incisors at the cingulum. When some incisors are un erupted, the arch wire should be placed lingual to the primary incisor in case the permanent incisors were to erupt lingual to the arch wire. The arch wire should be located 2mm below the gingival margin or edentulous ridge in the posterior regions to prevent distortion under forces of mastication. It should be located 1 to 2 mm lingual to the posterior teeth to permit satisfactory eruption of the bicuspids in a buccolingual plane. Impingement of the wire on soft tissues should be avoided. The arch wire should meet the band at the mesiobuccal cusp. By placing the soldered joint in the mid third of the band, interference with the gingival or with the occlusal fit of the band are eliminated.

Attachment of wire to bands

Wires are attached to the bands in two ways; by soldering or a locking system. The former one is called fixed lingual arch and the later one Fixed-Removable lingual arch.

Directly soldering wire to the bands has several advantages; the area of union can be smoothly contoured. Patients wearing this type of appliance over a long term tend to exhibit less tissue hypertrophy, and it is sturdier appliance requiring less supervision. Those arch wire that employ locking system are easier to insert, since the bands can be cemented individually, isolation from saliva is easier. These appliances are also easier to modify or to add a finger spring. If it is required in future stabilization with locks can be problematical with long-term wearing.

Second clinical visit[21]

The appliance is tried in the mouth of the patient, and any adjustments that are needed may be made so that the arch wire adapts precisely to the required points. Then the appliance is cemented in position.

Problems can be created by the use of mandibular arch wires. The appliance must always be checked for passivity to prevent undesirable movement of teeth. One method for checking the passivity is to try in the appliance, work dental floss between tissue and wire, and drag the floss between the wire and the incisor teeth. If the floss does not pass easily between teeth and wire, then the appliance very likely is active. **(Refer Chapter 17. Fig.5: Lingual arch space maintainer).**

Weldable Lingual arch space maintainer

CHAWLA et al in 1984 gave a modification of lingual arch space maintainer. According to them conventional lingual arch space maintainer given in cases of bilateral loss of deciduous molars, necessitates soldering of wire on the lingual side of bands and also canine spurs. With the present designs, the wire can be welded on the buccal side of the band instead of soldering the double back wire design provides sufficient strength. Also, the canine stoppers are made from the same wire thus simplifying the construction.[80]

PALATAL ARCH APPLIANCES

Palatal arch wires are designed to prevent mesial migration of the maxillary molars. They differ from mandibular lingual arch which not only prevents mesial migration but also the lingual collapse or tipping of incisor teeth.

Similar to the lingual arch wire, palatal arch wires are also constructed with at least 0.036-inch diameter wire.

1) NANCE PALATAL HOLDING ARCH

The Nance arch is simply a maxillary lingual arch that does not contact the anterior teeth, but approximates an acrylic button that contacts the palatal tissue, which theoretically provides resistance to the anterior movement of posterior teeth.[21]

Indication

Nance palatal arch is simply a maxillary 1st permanent molar positioning when there is bilateral premature loss of primary teeth, with no loss of space in arch and a favorable mixed dentition analysis.

If space maintenance is combined with habits like tongue thrusting etc. it is also used to break the habits by incorporating spurs in the acrylic button.

Construction

Bands are fitted to the maxillary molar teeth and impression is taken. Then the cast is made with bands on molar teeth. Palatal wire is soldered directly to the bands for stability. The arch wire extends anteriorly should not rest against the surfaces of the primary molars as the successor bicuspids usually are broader buccolingually, the wire could deflect them from their natural position.

At the rugae area, a small u-shaped bend should be incorporated in the wire, which is approximately 1-2 mm away from the soft tissue. This bend will enhance the retention of the acrylic to the wire.

The acrylic button is placed usually on the descending portion of the palatal vault the button is about 0.5 inch in diameter, rest against the palatal tissues. The button is intended to distribute forces over the palatal area so that the wire does not embed itself into the tissues.[60]**(Refer Chapter 17. Fig. 6: Nance palatal arch).**

Advantage

The appliance is effective space maintainer.

Disadvantage

Soft tissue irritation can be a problem. The acrylic portion can become embedded in the soft tissue if the palatal tissue hypertrophies because of poor oral hygiene or if the appliance is distorted.

2) TRANSPALATAL ARCH APPLIANCE

More recently, the transpalatal arch has been recommended for stabilizing the maxillary 1st permanent molars, when the primary molars require extraction. The appliance does not use an acrylic button. It seems to gain its efficiency through its rigidity. Although no studies have been published to demonstrate the efficacy of this appliance, it has been clinical observed to satisfactorily maintain the 1st permanent molars in position. **(Refer Chapter 17. Fig.7: Trans palatal arch).**

<u>**Indication**</u>

a) The best indication for transpalatal arch is when one side of the arch is intact, and several primary teeth on the other side are missing.[81]

b) It is also indicated when primary molars are lost bilaterally. However, there is a controversy that, both permanent molars may tip anteriorly despite the transpalatal arch, and in these cases a conventional lingual arch or Nance palatal holding arch is preferred.

c) The appliance is designed to prevent the molars from rotating around the palatal roots, which is the 1st movement resulting in loss of space in the arch perimeter.[73]

<u>**Construction**</u>

The construction of the transpalatal arch was described by **HILL et al** [1975] and **TSAMTSOURIS** and **GEORGE E .WHITE** [1977].[73]

The transpalatal arch runs directly across the palatal vault avoiding contact with the soft tissue. During the initial clinical procedure, the bands are fitted on the molar teeth. Impression is taken and cast is made with molar bands.

During the laboratory procedure, a 0.036 inch or 0.040-inch standard round wire Is bent to confirm to the palatal contour on the model and extending toward the palatal surface of the bands. As it approaches the mesial part of the palatal surface of the band, the wire should be bent to the distal part of the band to assure a better joint.

The wire should be spot welded to the band to assure a more accurate fit, followed by a solder joint at the junction of the molar band and the wire. Then the wire should be heat treated in order to be passive. Finally, the appliance should be polished and prepared for insertion.[28]

DISTAL SHOE SPACE MAINTAINER

The fixed distal shoe space maintainer, was first reported by **WILLETS [1932].** The appliance is constructed where there is a premature loss of second primary molar. This was a cast gold appliance and soon fell into disfavor due to the increased cost. The commonly used one is that described by **ROCHE [1942].** A crown or band and bar appliance. The major difference between the two appliances in the gingival extension. The Roche variety had a V- shaped gingival extension, while the wallets one had a bar type. Distal shoe appliance is also known as intra alveolar appliance.

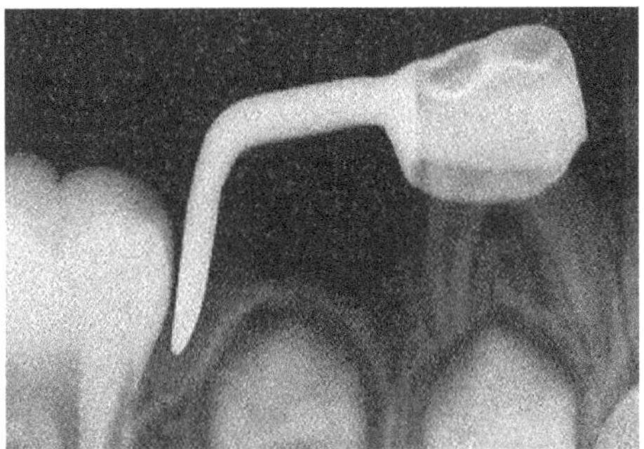

Fig.8: Radiograph showing the extension of loop

The distal surface of the second primary molar provides a guide for the un erupted 1st permanent molar. When the second primary molar is removed prior to the eruption of the first permanent molar, the intra alveolar appliance provides greater control of the path of the eruption of the un erupted tooth and prevents undesirable mesial migration.[82]

Indication

a) Distal shoe appliance is indicated, when the second primary molar is extracted or lost before the eruction of first permanent molar.

b) Causes of premature loss or extraction may be unsuccessful pulp therapy. Advanced resorption and periapical bone destruction, un restorable crown due to extensive carious destruction, Ectopic eruption of the first permanent molar or ankylosis.

<u>**Contraindication**</u>

    a) Inadequate abutment due to multiple loss of teeth.

    b) Poor oral hygiene or lack of parent and patient cooperation.

    c) Medically compromised patients, like congenital heart diseases, kidney problems, juvenile diabetes, history of rheumatic fever, generalized debilitation, and hemophilia.

    d) Congenitally missing first permanent molar [rare]

<u>CONSTRUCTION</u>

Using first primary molar as abutment the stainless-steel band is adopted. If the morphology of the tooth does not permit easy placement and adaptation of band then the tooth is prepared for stainless steel crown which

is carefully contoured and cemented. The stainless-steel crown provides a desirable contour for the placement of stainless-steel band.

The band is placed over the stainless-steel crown or abutment tooth. A compound impression is made, the band is removed and placed in the impression and a stone model is prepared.[83]

<u>Construction of loop</u>

The tissue bearing loop is then contoured with a 0.040-inch wire extending distally and into the prepared opening on the model. The free ends of the loop are soldered to the band or directly to the crown in some cases.

<u>Position and width of the distal extension</u>

The primary function of the distal shoe appliance is to provide a guide plane for the eruption path of the un erupted first permanent molar. To fulfill this purpose successfully, we should have an understanding of the normal paths of eruption of the maxillary and the mandibular first permanent molar.

The mandibular and maxillary first permanent molars differ markedly in their path of eruption. The normal path of the eruption of the mandibular first permanent molar is in a mesial and lingual direction, erupting against the distal surface of the second primary molar, using it as a buttress to guide itself into position. **(Refer Chapter 17, Fig.9: Intra alveolar appliance).**

In contrast the maxillary first permanent erupts in a distal and facial direction until it meets muscular resistance. It then erupts in a mesial direction until contact is made with the distal surface of the second primary molar.

Because the eruption pattern of the mandibular and maxillary 1st permanent molars differs, the design and the placement of the distal extension of the appliance will differ for upper and lower arches.

In the lower arch, the contact area of distal extension should have a slight lingual position over the crest of the alveolar ridge in order to engage the mesial contact area of the first permanent molar as it begins its mesial and lingual movements. By contrast, the contact area of the distal extension of the maxillary appliance should be slightly facial to the crest of the alveolar ridge. These considerations are important in preventing the erupting permanent molar from slipping contact with the appliance. An occlusal radiograph is helpful in checking the faciolingual placement of the gingival extension. There is also a tendency for the erupting first permanent molar to slip contact with the appliance when the width of the gingival extension is too narrow. The width should closely approximate the normal contact area of the distal surface of the second primary molar being replaced.[83]

Length of the distal extension [horizontal bar]

Determining the proper length of the distal extension can be simplified if the second primary molar is present, as it serves as a guide. Ideally, the molar should be retained until the appliance is ready for cementation.

If the second primary molar is already missing, it is recommended to measure on a radiograph, the distance between the distal surface of the first primary molar and the mesial surfaces of the un erupted first permanent molar. One problem may arise from relying entirely on this measurement. Since the developing crown of the first permanent molar, especially in the lower arch at three and four years of age, is normally in a more distal position prior to its eruption, the tooth could be forced to erupt too far distally.

In the lower arch an appliance constructed on the basis of the radiographic measurement alone could force the first permanent molar to erupt in a class II molar relationship. The best approach to determine the distal extent of the appliance when the second primary molar is missing to record the mesiodistal width of the opposite second primary molar if present and comparing that with the radiographic measurements. It is not necessary in all cases , therefore to extend the appliance to the mesial surface of the first permanent molar.[82]

Depth of the gingival extension [vertical bar]

Another determination to be made in constructing the appliance is the intra-alveolar depth of the gingival extension. If the extension is left too long, the possible harm to the developing second molar may result. If the extension is too short, the first permanent molar could erupt underneath the appliance. For indirect construction techniques, a good preoperative radiograph that is slightly under exposed to show the thickness of the overlying soft tissues will aid in determining the depth of the groove to be cut in the working model for constructing the gingival extension. The gingival extension of the appliance should be constructed to extend about 1 mm [hicks] below the mesial marginal ridge of the first permanent molar or just sufficient to capture its mesial surface on the tooth erupts and moves forward.[82]

APPLIANCE PLACEMENT

Next, the appliance is removed from the model and the V of the tissue extension is filled in and soldered with pieces of 0.040-inch wire. A knife edge is formed at the apex of the V, if the second primary molar has previously been extracted and the extraction side has healed. The sharpened distal shoe may be forced through a sterilized and anaesthetized area of the ridge. If the appliance is delivered at the time of extraction, the intragingival extension is just polished and not sharpened.

Before final placement of the maintainer in the mouth, a radiograph is taken to determine the tissue extension of the appliance is in proper relationship with the un erupted first permanent molar. Final adjustment in length and contour of the distal shoe can be made at this time.

For the case where the distal shoe is contraindicated, two possibilities for treatment exist;

1) To allow the tooth to erupt and regain the space later or.
2) Use a removable or fixed appliance that does not penetrate the tissue but pleases pressure on the ridge mesial to the unerupted permanent molar.

CARROLL and JONES have reported three cases in which a pressure appliance, removable or fixed was used to guide the permanent molar as it erupted.

According to **BARBER** the appliance has become controversial and has fallen into the disfavor in recent years. First there have been reports of trauma and damage to the un erupted permanent teeth by the appliance or procedures. Second it is felt that the normal eruption of the lower first permanent molar rarely contacts the root surfaces of the second deciduous molar and does not use the root for eruption guidance at all.

Instead, the lower first permanent molar normally erupts occlusal ward to contact first the distal crown surface of the deciduous molar and uses that to buttress for up righting and establishing a mesial position. In that case it is felt that an appliance is necessary only to relapse, and to stimulate, the distal crown surfaces of the lost deciduous molar.

In maxillary arch it is the only necessary to replace similarly the missing second deciduous molar crown with some form of distal extension, a loop a bar, or an acrylic tooth. Since the maxillary first permanent molar first erupts distally away from the arch until the cusp tips enter the mouth and then swings mesially to contact the distal crown surface of the deciduous molar it is not necessary to consider an appliance that inserts into the tissue.[84]

LEVIT [1971] shows an alternative method for construction of distal shoe space maintainer whereby the second deciduous molar is removable and the mesial root is ground off. Then the tooth is placed in a previously taken impression. After the stone has set, the deciduous molar with distal root is removed and the distal shoe is bent down to the distal surface of the artificial distal socket. This eliminates the need for some adjustments in mouth and some x-ray exposures.

Once the permanent molar has erupted, the space for the second molar has erupted, the space for the second premolar must be maintained for another three to four years; For the long haul, two bands and a bar are probably better than the single band and loop maintainer. We have to remember also that during this time period the first deciduous molar itself, with its band or crown, will probably be lost before the second premolar is ready to erupt. In these cases, the space maintainer is to be prepared by giving band to the first permanent molar and loop. A lingual arch space maintainer may also be given for those cases.[85]

BEAVER et al in 1967 described an appliance for molar guidance. In this case a stainless-steel crown is adapted to the abutment tooth. An impression is taken and the crown is transferred onto the cast. Buccal tubes [0.036 inch] are soldered on to the labial and lingual surfaces of the stainless-steel crown. The buccal tube is placed in horizontal plane and the lingual tube in a vertical position. Orthodontic wire [0.032] is adapted to the ridge where the deciduous second molar has been cut away from the cast with a laboratory knife. The wire is inserted into the buccal tube and the lingual portion is bent at right angles to fit into the vertical tube.

A lokfite wire is soldered to hold the loop in place. The distal alveolar shoe is then soldered to the wire, to guide the unerupted permanent molar into proper position.

The deciduous second molar is then extracted at a subsequent visit and the removable distal shoe is inserted, the appliance is inserted from the buccal side by placing the wire through the horizontal buccal tube, swinging the lingual portion into the vertical tube, and then locking the appliance in place.

After the permanent molar is fully erupted, it is advisable to remove the appliance and solder a loop on the occlusal surface of the wire to hold the permanent molar upright. An alternative appliance is a band and loop space maintainer with the band cemented to the permanent molar.86

PSALTIS and FISCHER in 1982 suggested an appliance for space maintenance and molar guidance.

A combination of lingual arch and distal shoe appliance was suggested for use in patients in whom both primary molars are lost. In treatment of a 4 ½ year old girl, the mandibular primary first molars and one primary second molar were extracted because they were unrestorable. The patients strong gag reflex prevented the use of a removable appliance.

A combination of appliance was designed to maintain in position the remaining primary second molar and provide guidance for the un erupted permanent molar on the opposite side. The right primary second molar was fitted with an orthodontic band, and the left primary canine was prepared for stainless steel crown. An orthodontic wire was placed and extended from the soldered lingual connection on the band to the canine in a fashion typical of a passive lingual arch wire. It was then extended back to the unerupted molar on both buccal and lingual sides of the edentulous alveolar ridge. The extension was soldered to the canine crown. A double bar was constructed to provide extra support for the long free ended extension.

The appliance was modified with removal of the buccal wire after some hyperplastic tissue appeared on the buccal mucosa. It was retained until both permanent molars had erupted, at which time all existing wires were cut from the canine crown and a passive lingual holding arch was placed.

The appliance is simple in design and construction and relative to other choices, inexpensive to the patient. Although the appliance provided no occlusion for opposing teeth, no over eruption of the maxillary molars occurred nor anticipated.[88]

CHAWLA et al (1985) suggested modifications of distal shoe space maintainer by placing loops in the horizontal arms of the space maintainer. These loops will permit the precise adjustments needed for accurate placement of the distal shoe against first permanent molar.

First in 1984, they suggested vertical loops and in 1985 horizontal loops instead of vertical which prevents impingement of gums pads sometimes noted with space maintainer having vertical loops.[80]

A case report of distal extension space maintenance utilizing a stainless-steel crown, welded sheath, and wire loop was given **by THEODORE P. CROLL in 1980.**

Maxillary 2nd deciduous molars were advised for extraction. It was decided to perform stainless steel crown restorations for the maxillary primary first molars and to attach stainless steel wires for distal extension intra alveolar space maintainers. The appliance was to be placed at the time of extraction of the respective primary second molars. A traditional stainless-steel crown and soldered wire was adapted and placed in two visits for the left side, with the use of local anesthesia.

With the intension of creating an adjustable appliance, it was planned to weld a horizontal sheath to the buccal aspect of the crown for the maxillary right primary first molar.[87]

Technique

a. An impression was taken and a model was poured in fast set plaster. The right second primary molar was cut off the model and a groove were sliced in the plaster bucco –lingually in the presumed location of the mesial aspect of the first permanent molar. Estimation of the permanent molar position was determined by radiographic measurement.

b. A 0.036 stainless steel wire was bent to extend from the welded sheath, across the edentulous span, submerging intra alveolarly with its distal end contoured around the mesial aspect of the first permanent molar. The wire included a loop in its course to facilitate ligation into the sheath and also to allow for adjustment of wire length if original estimation was inaccurate.

c. With anesthetic infiltration, the stainless-steel crown with the buccal sheath was adapted, but not cemented, on the right primary first molar.

d. The primary second molar was extracted and hemostasis was achieved with moistened gauze sponges. The second primary molar displayed complete destruction of the distobuccal root and advanced resorption of the remaining roots. The mesial aspect of the first permanent molar was observed in the extraction site.

e. The stainless-steel wire was inserted in to the sheath, ligated securely with 0.010 ligature wire, and the appliance was positioned and the prepared first primary molar. The wire extension proves to be too short but after several minor adjustments in length and position, the wire rested interalveolar against the first permanent molar. By clinical observation of the extraction site and radiographic measurement of second premolar, it was determined that the wire did not need to be activated for space regaining.

The course of healing was without complication and in six months – the maxillary first permanent molars were observed, erupted and maintained in proper position by the respective wires. At that time, a maxillary palatal holding arch appliance was fabricated.

The appliance in this case were designed to function as interim devices until the first permanent molars could be banded for a maxillary palatal holding arch appliance.[87]

SHERYL B. HUNTER in 1989, reported a case of space maintenance with the Garcia- Godoy appliance.

Garcia- Godoy's appliance consists of a stainless-steel wire extending distally from the buccal and lingual surfaces of the deciduous first molar. The U Loop extended on each side across the edentulous span, submerging subgingivally, and one small loop on each side contacts the mesial surface of the permanent molar.

FIXED APPLIANCE FOR MAINTENANCE OF PRIMARY INCISOR

Fixed bridges and cast overlays:

Described by MC DONALD and AVERY. In the past, fixed bridges and the cast gold overlays and loop were sometimes used for space maintenance in the primary incisor area. Now the economic considerations of both dentist and patient usually preclude the use of gold appliances. If a fixed appliance is required, one approach is to attach the anterior replacement teeth to a 0.040- or 0.045-inch stainless steel wire frame work retained with bands or crowns on the secondary primary molars if the first primary molars are present an indirect retainer may be placed on the occlusal area to prevent the wire from flexing. Additional stabilization can be obtained by using a Nance button covering the ridge with dental acrylic resin.[88]

Esthetic anterior space maintainers:

It was described by **STEFFEN J. B.** and **JOHNSON. R. in 1971.** A simple method of constructing a space maintainer also provides an esthetic component. The space maintainer also consists of a plastic tooth processed onto a lingual arch which, in turn, is attached to bands for the molars.

A shade and a poly carbonate or acrylic tooth are selected. Stainless steel bands or crowns are fitted to the deciduous second molars, preferably, and an impression is made with the bands in place. The bands or crowns are secured in the impression and the latter is poured in stone.

An arch is constructed of either 0.036 inch or 0.040-inch wire, and fitted to rest at the base of the cingulum. Elgiloy is preferred to chrome steel wire.

An attachment post is prepared from 0.028-inch wire and soldered to the lingual arch in the site of the missing tooth. The post wire should be placed so that it will lie in the middle of the replacement tooth when the replacement tooth is set in the arch on the model. The post wire should be looped around the lingual arch, tightened, and held in place while it is being soldered. Adjoining teeth should be covered with clay and a double thickness of aluminium foil, to prevent damage during the soldering.

After the soldering, the post is bent incisally to confirm to the curvature of the arch, and in a loop about half the height of the adjacent incisors. The loop in the wire acts to retain the tooth.65

The appliance is removed from the model and polished. The plastic tooth is contoured to the gingiva and positioned in the arch. The tooth is prepared to receive the post. When the tooth is on the post in the proper position, it is ready for processing with fast setting acrylic resin. The model is coated with liquid foil to prevent the acrylic from adhering to the stone model.

After processing, the tooth is trimmed to pontic form and polished. It is now ready for insertion in the mouth for final adjustment.

The appliance has proved to be adjustable and practical. As many as these teeth have been replaced successfully with this space maintainer. The appliance can be made fitted for about the same cost as the removable acrylic appliance and for considerably less than a cast partial denture. The appliance is contraindicated in patients with closed bite, because the artificial tooth cannot be positioned properly in such patients.[65]

Esthetic self-adjusting anterior space maintainer

An esthetic self-adjusting appliance for anterior space maintenance was described by ROBERTS in 1971.

The continual development of the inter canine distance in the deciduous dentition demonstrates that this growth must not be restricted by fixed devices. Consequently, the ideal esthetic space maintainer for prematurely lost deciduous incisors should also permit growth and development of the anterior component.

The use of stainless-steel bands attached to the deciduous molars as abutments offer the advantage of being easily adapted without the necessary of tooth reduction or compromise of anterior esthetics which would result with anterior tooth banding. After adaptation of bands to the deciduous molars, a white compound with a hot spatula, and poured in plaster.

After separation, a no. 0.040 stainless steel wire is adapted on the cast in two sections. One section stops at the mesial surface of the deciduous canine. A no 0.040 round tube is then soldered to the end of the wire crossing lingual to the remaining incisors.

The second section of wire from the opposite side is contoured, with the anterior section left straight from the mesial surface of the primary canine on one side of the arch and extending into the buccal tube on the opposite side. A small loop, spur, or wire is soldered to the arch wire in the region of the tooth to be replaced, aiding in the retention of the acrylic tooth. This replacement tooth can be easily fabricated using a small acrylic denture tooth and attached to the wire with tooth-colored cold-curing acrylic resin. After proper contouring and polishing, the appliance is ready for cementation.[81]

FABRICATION OF A MORE DURABLE FIXED ANTERIOR ESTHETIC APPLIANCE

Jean R. Jasmine and John N. Groper (1984) described fabrication of a more durable fixed anterior esthetic appliance. The authors described two techniques, one utilizing an open-faced stainless-steel crown and the other utilizing a solid direct bond pad with a mesh base.[81] **(Refer Chapter 17, Fig.10: Groper's appliance).**

Technique utilizing an open-faced stainless-steel crown:

a. Pedodontic stainless steel crowns or pedodontic molar bands (unitek) are adapted to the maxillary first or second primary molars. The tooth shade is selected.

b. Alginate impressions of the upper and lower arches are taken with the stainless-steel crown's bands in place on the teeth and the impressions are poured in stone. A wax bite is made in centric occlusion.

c. Anterior stainless-steel crowns are selected to fit edentulous space.

d. Using sticky wax on the labial aspects of the anterior stainless-steel crowns, the crowns are fixed in the position on the stone model. The conclusion with the lower model is checked.

e. An 0.036 or 0. 040 stainless steel wire is adapted to the lingual surfaces of the maxillary teeth, including the anterior stainless-steel crowns.

f. The lingual wire is soldered to the posterior stainless-steel crowns or bands and to the anterior stainless-steel crowns.

g. The labial faces of the anterior stainless-steel crowns are removed and the edge of the crowns are bent inwards to create retentive areas.

h. An opaquer may be used at this stage to block out the stainless-steel color. A self-curing resin is then placed in the open-faced stainless-steel crowns.

i. The acrylic is trimmed and polished. The rest of the appliance is removed from the stone model and polished.

j. The appliance is cemented in position.[81]

SOME OTHER FIXED SPACE MAITAINERS

BAR TYPE SPACE MAITAINER

HINRICHSEN (1962) described about the bar type nonfunctional fixed space maintainer. **(Refer Chapter 17, Fig.11: Band and Bar)**

A bar is attached to the mesial aspect of a crown or band on the 2nd deciduous molar or 1st permanent molar or on the distal aspect of the 1st deciduous molar, and it may take the following forms:

a) A bar touching the next tooth in the arch, thus restoring the former contact point.

b) A bar bent into an "S "shape before touching the next tooth.

c) A bar is attached to the next tooth through a ring soldered to a band or crown.

d) A bar which passes into a tube soldered to a band or crown on the next tooth or vice versa; this may be activated to reopen space by threading a coil spring over the bar and activating it between the tube and a stop placed on the bar.

e) A bar incorporating a screw to reopen space

f) The "Wesoke bar-maintainer". This passes bar into a hole cut for if in a proximal amalgam restoration. After the bar is placed, the slot is packed around the bar with amalgam.

g) The coil spring – ligature space-maintainer. Thick ligature wire is looped around the gingival margin of one deciduous molar and the two ends of the ligature are passed through a tubular coil spring cut to the length of the space, then ligated around the adjacent tooth at its gingival margin.[81]

ADJUSTABLE SPACE MAINTAINER FOR

THE GENERAL PRACTIONER

It was described by **JOSEPH J. SCHACHTER in 1963.** This does not require preparation of abutment teeth, impression, soldering or special instruments. It can be inserted in one visit and is adjustable to all spaces.

Procedure

To insert the space maintainer the band is fitted with the tubes towards the edentulous area. The technique of fitting the band no different than usual procedure. Care must be taken to fit all occlusal edges of the band below the

occlusal level of the tooth. The width of the edentulous area is then measured and a space loop is selected that is slightly smaller than the area measured.

The band is removed and the vertical post of the space loop are inserted through the tubes from the occlusal surface. The free ends of the posts are bent through 90 degrees toward the center of the gingival edge of the band, locking the space loop in place. The band and space loop are cemented to place. After the cement has dried, the final adjustment is made by increasing the size of the loops.

A No.139 plier is used to increase the length of the space loop. The square end is placed in the hallow of the convolutions, both buccal and lingual. As the plier is tightened the length of the loop increases, causing the distal portion to touch the adjacent tooth **below** the contact point. This position prevents the loop from moving occlusally. An increase in length upto 1 mm may be obtained in this manner.

Other adjustments may be made with ease. The step-down portion of loop affords further increase or decrease in length. The direction of the distal portion may be made by adjustment at this portion of the loop and special sizes must be made before the cementation of the band. The loop is first locked into place and the space maintainer is fitted into the mouth for adjustment in length is made only after cementation.

<u>MODIFIED LOOP APPLIANCE</u>

The loop, maintaining the space that it occupies, is simplified design is given by **MATHEWSON.** It is similar to an appliance advocated by **MAYNE W.R. [GRABER 1972].** Its design is uncomplicated and is easily adaptable to the direct one- sitting procedure as to the indirect, two –sitting technique. The appliance consists of a stainless-steel band or crown as the anchor for the L-shaped inter proximal bracing.[90] **(Refer Chapter 17, Fig.12: Mayne's Appliance).**

<u>Procedure</u>

<u>Direct method [single sitting]</u>

   a. Carefully trim, adapt, polish and place a stainless steel.

   b. Obtain a 5 cm length of 0.036 round wire.

   c. Place the beaks of a no.139 pliers about 8 mm from the end of the wire and make a 45-degree bend.

d. Place the beaks of a no.139 pliers about 2mm beyond the first bend and bend again, returning it to its original bearing. This 2 mm bend locates or otherwise straight segment of wire adjacent to the gingival tissue.

e. With the bend directed gingivally, flatten both sides of the 8 mm section using a mounted stone or abrasive disc.

f. Holding the wire in the same position using a three jaw pliers, place a gentle curve in the 8 mm section corresponding to the convexity of the buccal surface of the crowned or banded tooth.

g. Remove the crown or band from the tooth and place the wire in position and back weld.

h. Replace the spot-welded crown or band unit on the anchor tooth and check the wire for alignment. The gingival band should be adjacent to the proximal surface of the tooth. The wire should extend along the gingival tissue.

i. Remove the crown or band unit and flame or electro solder the spot weld.

j. Smooth and polish the solder joint, Using Pumice and rag wheel, gold range and rag wheel.

k. Replace the crown or band unit on the anchor tooth and with a white pencil place a mark even with the distal surface of the canine.

l. Make a right-angled bend by placing the beak of the no.139 pliers at the white mark placing the bend distal to the canine.

m. Using the wire cutter, clip off excess, leaving about 4mm of wire beyond the distolingual area of the canine.

n. With the no.800-413 three jaw pliers, place two tends in the right-angle section.

    I) a concave bend to allow wire to conform to distal curvature of the distal surface of the canine and

    II) a concave bend to conform to the curvature of the gingival.

More minor adjustments will adapt the right-angle section comfortably in place.

o. Finish and polish the appliance.

p. Cementation of the appliance.[90]

Indirect Method:

a. Adapt the stainless-steel crown or band to the tooth.

b. Compound or alginate impression with the crown or band in place. Pour the stone model.

c. Cement temporary crown coverage for the prepared primary molar with the thin mixture of zinc oxide-eugenol cement.

d. Adapt and contour the L Loop.

e. Anchor the L loop in place at the canine area using a mix of stone or investment and then flame solder it to the crown or band.

f. Smooth, polish and cement the space maintainer.[90]

FUNCTIONAL MAINTENANCE OF ARCH LENGTH

NORMAN P. MARTINEZ and HENRY G. ELSBACH [1984] introduced a technique to maintain arch length utilizing a fixed functional space maintainer that can be constructed by the direct or indirect method.

Indication

a. When the space for a permanent tooth should be maintained for two years or longer.

b. To avoid supra eruption of a tooth from the opposing arch.

c. To improve the physiology of a child's masticatory system and restore dental health optimally.

<u>**Contraindication**</u>

As for all other space maintainers are best made utilizing stainless steel crown as retainers. Using stainless steel crown as retainers. Using stainless steel crowns prevents recurrence of caries, which is very important in children with high caries susceptibility. It also simultaneously restores the tooth.[27]

<u>MEHODS FOR CONSTRUCTION OF A FIXED FUNCTIONAL SPACE MAINTAINER</u>

1.<u>Indirect technique</u>

a) The patient is examined occlusion is checked and the need for a space maintainer is determined.

b) The abutment teeth are prepared for steel crowns. The preparation consists of a 1.5 mm occlusal reduction, proximal slices, and a small amount of buccal and lingual reduction except for permanent teeth.

c) Stainless steel crowns are adapted to the abutment teeth. Crowns are crimped as necessary to get a tight fit and retention.

d) Compound impression is taken for the quadrant with the crowns in mouth. The crowns are placed in compound and secured and model is poured.

e) When the model has been poured, a stainless-steel crown is selected for pontic, trimmed as needed and placed on model.

f) Pontic is soldered to abutment teeth and the space maintainer.

g) The pontic is crimped wherever necessary and filled with self-curing acrylic and cemented into place.[27]

2. Direct Technique

a. Double Abutment Type

a) The patient is examined, occlusion is checked and need for space maintainer is determined.

b) The abutment teeth (teeth adjacent to space) are prepared for a stainless-steel crown.

c) Stainless steel crowns are adapted for abutment teeth.

d) A two-centimeter piece of 0.030 Blue Eligiloy wire is taken and spot welded to the buccal, occlusal gingival middle third of the distal stainless steel crown molar.

e) The wire is bent to confirm to the curve of the arch and cross the buccal middle third of the canine. The wire is marked where it crosses the canine with a wax pencil.

f) The pencil marks are used to relate wire to canine in the welder and the wire is spot welded to the canine crown. The stainless-steel crowns with wire are tried in to check fit. After fit has been confirmed, it is made sure that welds are secure.

g) Pontic is selected to fit space, trimmed as necessary, related to wire and marked with wax pencil. The pontic is spot welded to wire and the space maintainer is tried in.

h) Another place of two-centimeter 0.030 blue Elgiloy wire is taken and spot welded to the lingual surfaces of all three stainless steel crown. After trying in the space maintainer and checking the fit, all the welded areas are soldered and the space maintainer is polished.

i) The pontic is crimped if necessary and filled with self-curing acrylic and cemented in place.[27]

b. <u>Cantilever type</u>

a) The clinical case is seen, occlusion is checked and the need for space maintainer is determined.

b) In this case there is no preparation for a stainless-steel crown on the abutment tooth because a 1st permanent molar is used. Stainless steel crown is adapted and crimped as necessary. A stainless-steel crown is selected as a pontic and one-half centimeter piece of 0.030 Blue Eligiloy wire is spot welded to the mesial surface and bent at a right angle to make occlusal rest on first primary molar, and excess wire is cut off if necessary. The pontic is related to stainless steel crown abutment and marked with wax pencil. Stainless steel crown abutment and pontic are oriented on spot welder with pencil marks. The space maintainer is welded and tried- in.

c) Wire occlusal rest is soldered to pontic and pontic to abutment crowns and polished if necessary. Cold cure acrylic resin is placed in the pontic and cemented in place.[27]

<u>CEMENTATION OF APPLIANCE</u>

The teeth must be prepared by fluoride and cavity varnish before the bands are placed. The child's teeth are cleaned with a fluoride mix in the pumice material, and a fluoride gel or equivalent is applied, for the time suggested by the manufacturer. The child's teeth are then washed and air dried and cotton rolls are placed to maintain a dry field. This surface coating varnish prevents any acid etching from the freshly applied zinc phosphate cement.

Teeth treated in this fashion are also extremely resistant to enamel etching due to accumulation, which sometimes is seen to occur along the margin of the bands in the mouth of the child who is not on a good regimen of oral health care at home. When bands are worn , tooth brushing procedures must be constantly reinforced by the dentist.[92]

Materials needed

1. Appliance to be cemented.
2. Large, round amalgam plugger.
3. Large amalgam carrier.
4. Any type of zinc phosphate cement.
5. Chilled glass slab.
6. Thin bladed cement spatula.

Procedure

a) The dental assistant mixes a thick, shiny mix of zinc phosphate cement on a chilled glass slab with a thin- bladed metal spatula completely fills the bands of the appliance, from the gingival side and passes to the dentist.

b) The dentist presses the band onto the teeth with the index finger as far as possible and then firmly seats the band, using alternating pressures around the margins with the large round amalgam plugger. As the band is pressed into the place, cement should be forced out around the gingival margin.

c) While the cement is setting, burnish the margins of the band against the tooth with some pressure, using the side of the amalgam plugger. This prevents fat- edged bands and an open cement margin, which invites loosening and the initiation of the hypo calcified enamel along the margin.

d) After the appliance has been cemented in this fashion, allow the cement to set for 5 minutes, maintaining a dry field. Then scuff away the excess cement with carrier blade.[92]

CROLL T. P [1983] discussed about the cementation of stainless-steel space maintaining appliances is a critical out often poorly managed part of space maintenance procedures. This article describes a method of adapting and cementing a fixed unilateral stainless steel space maintainer and gives recommendations for follow up.[93]

A small strips of autoclave masking tape is pressed over the occlusal surface of the band, and a creamy mix of cement is placed inside. The band is filled about three-quarters full. An explorer or cement spatula is used to spread the cement over the entire interior of the band. The appliance is positioned in the tooth, first with the finger pressure and then with the band pusher. The masking tape serves to force the cement gingivally and ensure that voids does not occur between the tooth and band as a result of the occlusal escape of the cement.

After the appliance is completely seated the tape is removed and final seating adjustments are made with the band pusher. The patient is instructed to bite firmly on a folded 2 x 2-inch cotton gauze until the cement is set. The cotton is then removed from the tooth with much of the hardened cement entrapped in the gauze. Cement removal is completed with a curette, explorer, and ultrasonic sealer.[93]

12. Bonded Space Maintainers

Space maintenance is usually a multivisit procedure requiring banding, impression taking and several laboratory procedures for fixed maintainers prior to seating and cementation. Various problems such as loosening of bands, decalcification of abutment teeth, irritation to oral tissues etc. can be encountered with these appliances.

With the use of acid etch technique and either ultra violet or chemically curing composite systems, simple space maintainers can be more readily made and retained with overall better gingival health to the tissue around the abutment teeth. Moreover, it is applied with less cost to the patient. **(Refer Chapter 17, Fig.13: Bonded space maintainer).**

If the principles of bonding composite to enamel are followed carefully, the bond will last for months or years necessary for holding the space prior to eruption of the permanent succedaneous tooth. The bonded unit will be very stable and will eliminate the problem of loop slipping below the contact point of abutment tooth or of chronic loss of appliance.

One of the first acid etch space maintainers attempted is a preformed loop of 0.81 mm [0.032] wire designed for spot welding onto the bands or stainless steel crowns, was bonded to a deciduous cuspid for the maintenance of first deciduous molar extraction space.[78]

Terence J. Swaine and Gerald Z. Wright (1976) evaluated a unilateral space maintainer using acid conditioning and direct bonding. Over six months, it showed a 70% success rate in preventing rotations and space loss, supporting further study. Directly bonded space maintainers on buccal surfaces appear effective for maintaining single-tooth spaces.[90]

SIMONSEN R. J. [1978] used a metal bar [3M company] in an attempt to improve the quality of and ease of adapting the bonding metal. The metal bar had two perforations at each end of a 20 mm long strip of stainless steel, 0.48 mm thick and 2 mm wide. This stainless-steel strip is preferable to a 0.032 wire for several reasons;

1. The strip is easier to adapt, particularly to short clinical crowns.

2. The strip, having a width of 2mm, cannot be inadvertently bent by a sharp chewing force.

3. The strip is thinner [0.48 mm] than 0.032 wire [0.81], thus allowing less bulky bands.[78]

Adaptations of the strip

A three – jaw wire bending plier is excellent for making the necessary bends at the end of the strip in order for the strip to conform to the buccal or lingual anatomy of the abutment teeth. To avoid occlusal interference, it is frequently desirable to bond maxillary strips to buccal surfaces, and mandibular strips to lingual surfaces even though this makes access more difficult in the mandibular quadrants. The space maintainer will work equally well buccally or lingually. If esthetics are of importance, a lingually placed space maintainer is best.

The strip is contoured to the tooth anatomy to ensure uniform composite thickness, which is crucial for effective bonding, as emphasized by **Buonocore (1975)** in orthodontic bracket adhesion. Compared to 0.032 wire, 3M stainless steel strips offer better uniformity and adaptability. For short clinical crowns, the strip can be trimmed without compromising strength or retention, minimizing gingival irritation.[94]

Bonding

Cotton rolls and saliva ejector [particularly for mandibular lingual bonding] were used for isolation. Use or rubber dam, however, invariably makes isolation much easier.

Enamel surfaces to be etched were pumiced to remove plaque and enamel pellicle. A rubber prophylaxis cup is adequate for smooth surface cleaning, although a brush may be needed on surfaces containing a groove, such as the buccal surface of the mandibular first permanent molars.

Only the tooth surfaces to be bonded are etched initially (to prevent contamination of the second tooth surface during moulding of the first tooth). After etching permanent enamel for 60 seconds, and deciduous enamel for 120 seconds (with 37% orthophosporic acid), and through washing and drying, 3M concise brand enamel bond was applied to the etched surface. Concurrently the filled composite concise was mixed and then applied around the ends of the wire and also on the top of the enamel bond layer. The wire was then held in place with lockable cotton pliers, until material at set. The strip could be more accurately placed and more firmly held in place during bonding, if one band was done at a time. Thus, the technique has been utilized of bonding the most accessible tooth first.

The second tooth can be etched and completed in a similar fashion. Applying the acid and resin layer to the second tooth surface must be done carefully to assure penetration of both acid and resin to all enamel surfaces under the metal strip. The perforated ends of the strip make this easier, as well as aiding in retention.

Any excessive bulk of composite can be easily trimmed, using a high speed fluted composite finishing bur. Particularly attention was made to the composite towards the gingival in order to eliminate any gingival irritation from composite flash. A glaze layer of 5 % sub-micron filled resin was applied, after washing and drying, to provide a smoother surface for tongue or cheek tissues.[95]

LINGUAL AND TRANSPALATAL ARCH

SIMONSEN also described about bonded lingual and transpalatal arches.[78]

Adapting lingual arch wires into grooves on first permanent molars, and then etching and bonding them in place, also eliminates the use of orthodontic bands and laboratory fees in these space maintainers. A study model is taken and 0.032 wire is adapted as needed. For maxillary transpalatal arches, the ends of the wire are adapted into the occluso-lingual groove, which provides against occlusal stresses for the space maintainer. For mandibular lingual arches, it is convenient to adapt the wire into the lingual groove and carrying it 2-3 mm down the groove towards the central fossa.

This will aid in retention as the wire will be supported against occlusal forces by the occlusal bend. The wire should be adapted along the middle 1/3 rd of the lingual surface, making certain to keep it away from the gingival margin to avoid irritation from the composite bond.

After adaptation on the cast, the arch can be bonded to the abutment teeth. It is easier to bond one tooth at a time. In the maxilla it is simply accomplished by holding the wire in position on one tooth while bonding the other tooth.

In the mandibular arch, saliva ejectors are excellent for restraining the tongue, as well as removing saliva. It has been found beneficial to mix a little impression material or compound impression material first and use this to hold lingual arch wire temporarily to the lower anterior teeth. This can be removed or cut away easily after the permanent molars are bonded.

Removal of the bond is simply accomplished by grinding the composite to the wire, pulling of the wire, and then with a high –speed fluted composite finishing bur, gradually removing all of the composites down to the enamel surface. Using the high-speed dry, it is clearly seen when the last layer of the composite is removed and the tooth enamel is reached.[78]

ARTUM and MARSTRANDER [1983] found that a round, multi strand orthodontic wire [0.032-inch diameter] to be more satisfactory than ordinary round wire, and they used an auto polymerizing composite resin. The main reason for the difference was thought to be the fact that the thick spiral wire allowed less bulk [and then less occlusal interference] and was easier to individualize.[95]

ANTERIOR SPACE MAINTAINER

BAYARDO discussed a case involving loss of maxillary left primary incisor in which direct bonding is used for space maintenance.

Two 0.018 x 0.025 edgewise standard buccal tubes were adapted to the mesio distal diameter of the right central and left lateral incisors. A stainless-steel mesh was spot welded to the tubes and trimmed at the base. A piece of rectangular 0. 018 x 0. 025 standard wire was bent u shaped, making sure that the wire touched the mesial surface of the abutment teeth. A polycarbonate crown was used as a pontic, and the palatal surface was grooved, to confirm to the wire. The crown and wire were fixed with composite.

The space maintainer was tried in patients mouth and was bonded to the abutment teeth using acid etch technique and self-curing composite.[97]

13. Removable Space Maintainers

Removable space maintainers are the appliance designed for easy removal for cleansing and adjustment. The advantages and disadvantages of removable appliances were discussed previously.

Removable acrylic appliances, used to hold the space, have a limited place in the daily practice. In a four-year study involving 226 space maintainers, only four [2 %] were of removable type **[HILL et al, 1975]**. None of the four appliances were present at the end of six months; two were lost, one broken, and one has presumed lost because of migration of the child from that place. This high failure rate demonstrates the problems in using removable appliances in children. The need to make an accurate preoperative assessment of the child's cooperative ability to wear the appliance is essential. [28]

Indications

Removable dentures are indicated when

1. Aesthetic is of importance.
2. The abutment teeth cannot support a fixed appliance, because of
     a. expected early loss, due to normal root resorption.
     b. previous injury or extended caries which has involved the pulp.
3. A cleft palate is to be closed with a denture.
4. Radiographs reveal that the unerupted permanent teeth over which the denture will be placed have not assumed a position from which they will erupt in less than 6 months.
5. The child has reached a mental age of 2 ½ years.
6. All the teeth has erupted.
7. The permanent teeth are not fully erupted for the adaptation of bands.
8. Multiple loss of deciduous teeth.[24]

Contraindications

1. Lack of patient – parent cooperation.
2. If the child has not attained a mental age of 2 ½ years.
3. If the patient is allergic to acrylic materials.
4. Epileptic patients.
5. Children with possible caries activity.

Classification

Removable appliance may be;

- Functional
- Nonfunctional
- With clasps
- Without clasp

Functional space maintainers will incorporate teeth to aid in mastication, speech and esthetics whereas in nonfunctional appliances will have only an acrylic extension over the edentulous area to prevent space closure.[21] **BRAUER et al** classified removable dentures for children as follows;

Class-1. Unilateral maxillary posterior.

Class-2. Unilateral mandibular posterior.

Class-3. Bilateral maxillary posterior.

Class -4. Bilateral mandibular posterior.

Class -5. Bilateral maxillary anterior posterior.

Class-6. Bilateral mandibular anterior posterior.

Class -7. One or more primary or permanent anteriors.

Class -8. Complete primary.[24]

<u>**Components of removable appliances**</u>

Removable appliances usually incorporate,

- ✓ an acrylic plate with extensions onto the edentulous space,

- ✓ clasps for extensions onto the edentulous space,

- ✓ clasps for retention occlusal rests if first permanent molars are to be clasped and

- ✓ acrylic teeth if the appliance is functional.

- ✓

<u>**Impression taking**</u>

A good full impression of the required jaw is taken. If functional space maintainer is required upper and lower impressions are made. Cast are poured with dental stone or plaster.

<u>**Fabrication of the space maintainer**</u>

DOUGLAS J. SANDERS [1958] discussed about the fabrication of acrylic space maintainer.

The use of self- curing acrylic resins has made the fabrication of the space maintainers a relatively simple procedure.

The materials needed to construct acrylic space maintainers consists of self- curing acrylic resin [monomer and polymer], squeeze bottles, medicine dropper bottle, separating liquid, 0.025-gauge stainless steel wire, wire cutters and pliers.

To construct a lower bilateral space maintainer, alginate impressions of both arches are taken in rim locked trays. A wax bite is taken for proper cast orientation and both impressions are poured in dental stone.

A serrated office pliers and 0.025-gauge stainless steel wire are used to adapt clasps around the deciduous cuspids. The anterior portion of the clasp is brought into inter proximal area to assure maximum retention. Rests made from 0.025-gauge wire are adapted to the mesial fossa of the first permanent molar, they provide stability of the denture.[30]

Both the clasps and the rests have their opposite ends bend into pigtails to assure retention in the acrylic resin. Space is left between the arms of the clasps and the rests and the casts so that the clasps and rest will not bear directly on the tissue. They are held in place by sticky wax on the labial and occlusal surfaces.

A large camel's – hair brush is used to apply liquid separating medium over all areas to be covered by acrylic resin. Small amounts of polymer powder are applied from a plastic squeeze bottle. The polymer is saturated with the monomer which is added from a medicine dropper. The acrylic resin is gradually built up in this manner until the saddle regions will be in occlusion with opposite arch. If the teeth are used in space maintainer [for functional maintenance] they should be arranged by keeping upper and lower models in occlusion. The lingual region is covered and the acrylic resin is placed in the inter proximal regions for added retention.

After the denture has set [preferably overnight] , it is trimmed and polished in the usual manner with vulcanite stones and with cotton wheels impregnated first with pumice and next with whiting .And the denture is now ready for the patient.[30]

<u>**CONSTRUCTION OF SPACE MAINTAINERS WITHOUT BANDS**</u>

HITCHCOCK has described about the construction of removable, functional, passive space maintainers. He said the construction should be as simple as possible. It is time saving to the dentist and the lower cost makes the benefit of the service available to more people.[8]

The labial Bow

Often a simple labial bow is the only wire bending involved. This aids in keeping the appliance in the mouth, and in the upper jaw keeps the anterior teeth from moving forward.

Other things being equal, in a case with normal jaw relation and a deep or medium overbite, a labial bow is not necessary in a lower space maintainer. Forward migration of the lower anterior teeth will be inhibited by the lingual surfaces of the maxillary anteriors.

Because the labial bow is used for retention, it should be for enough toward the gingival to accomplish this, should not impinge on the inter dental papillae. The passage of the wire from labial to lingual may pose some problem. Usually, it can go in the occlusal embrasure between the lateral incisor and the cuspid, or distal to the cuspid. Ordinarily, if the labial bow includes the incisors, the sufficient retention is obtainable. Cases arise, however in which there will be occlusal interference by the wire. Examinations of model or natural teeth in occlusion, may indicate that it would be better to bend the wire directly over the cusp of the canine and follow closely the lingual ridge on the upper model, or the labial ridge on the lower. This is possible where the lingual ridge on the upper canine is opposite to the labial embrasure in the lower arch or the labial ridge of a lower canine is opposite a lingual embrasure in the upper arch, when the teeth are in occlusion. The problem of fitting the wire is also a function of the size of the wire used.

Ordinarily 0.032 or 0.028 chrome nickel wire will be used. If the occlusal interference is a problem, 0.026 stainless steel wire, may be used. It is harder to bend than the Nichrome so it will not distort as easily and a smaller size may be used.

Occlusal rests

The item of complexity would be the addition of occlusal rests on the molars. These may be advisable in the lower jaw even though a labial bow is not used.[8]

Interproximal spurs

After occlusal rests would come interproximal spurs for additional retention. molar the lower, retention is not usually a problem, but owing to the child's constant playing with his tongue or inability to keep the maintainer in while eating, a labial bow and interproximal spurs may be necessary, as well as occlusal rests.

Clasps

Progressively complex are clasps. Clasps may be simple or of the modified crozat type where space maintenance is involved, the more complicated, super retentive, modified crozat is not usually necessary. Simple clasp may be interproximal clasps or wrap around clasps. Interproximal clasps crossover the occlusal embrasure from the lingual acrylic and terminate by means of a loop in the buccal embrasure. Because of tooth contour, the wrap-around clasp should be usually terminates with its free end to the mesial surface. Axial inclination and other possible factors may influence one to let the free end be distal.

Exclusive of retention, there is another reason for using or not using clasps. This involves the buccal – lingual relationship of opposing teeth. The presence of acrylic as only the lingual aspect of a tooth will often make this tooth move buccally.

A case was discussed by **Dr. ERNEST   SCHWARTZ [1978]** to illustrates the use of a clasp less partial denture to maintain space within the arch and between the arches, while restoring function, esthetics and phonetics for a young patient with multiple maxillary anterior deciduous teeth missing.

The case involved a 5-year-old boy in whose mouth, rampant caries left only the deciduous canines and right second deciduous molar salvageable in the maxillary arch. His mandibular teeth were unable to be restored within the condition, the young child was embarrassed to speak, laugh or smile.[5]

An immediate partial denture was fabricated and inserted by the oral surgeon upon removal of all root fragments and unsalvageable deciduous molars. Esthetics was restored with plastic deciduous teeth with natural diastemas in the incisor region. Posterior vertical dimension was restored with acrylic bite blocks.

The patient's acceptance of the appliance was immediate, accompanied by the ability to smile freely.

Clasp less removable appliances have been readily accepted by the children as young as 3 years old and are preferable because clasp usually enhance plaque built up in a caries prone mouth.

Fitting molar bands on partially erupted first permanent molars is challenging, especially in caries-prone mixed dentition, as it increases the risk of decalcification and caries. While lingual arches preserve space, they don't restore function, phonetics, or deglutition. The appliance used here is a cost-effective alternative that restores function and esthetics while supporting phonetics. As teeth erupt, acrylic can be trimmed to accommodate them. Molar stops on the lower appliance prevent overseating, and a horseshoe-shaped 0.030 wire embedded in acrylic enhances strength.[88]

REMOVABLE APPLIANCES FOR PRIMARY INCISOR AREA

Acrylic partial denture can be used successfully in primary incisor area[88], usually in maxillary arch. This type of appliances can be given if there is degree of cooperation and interest in the children. These should not be in children's mouth who have the possibility of caries activity.

REMOVABLE APPLIANCES FOR MULTIPLE LOSS OF TEETH

1.Acrylic partial denture

The acrylic partial denture has been used successfully after the multiple loss of the teeth in the mandible of the maxillary arch. This appliance can be readily adjusted to allow for the eruption of the teeth.

If artificial teeth are included in the denture, masticatory function can be restored. To minimize the breakage of the appliance anteriorly by the use of a stainless-steel lingual bar.

A partial denture of contoured cast type is acceptable due to the simplicity of construction, functional requirements, and cost to the patient. Retention of the appliance is important, particularly during the initial period of insertion. Stainless steel wire clasps can be contoured to primary canines and molars. Sometimes occlusal rests or molars and ball clasps can be given interdentally. If the permanent incisors are in an active state or eruption, the clasp should be removed after the child has become accustomed to wearing the appliance to allow distal drifting and lateral movement of the primary canines and alignment of the permanent incisors.it is unlikely that there is additional inter canine expansion in the older child. Therefore, no adverse effect on the dental arch can follow the fixation of primary canines with clasp before the eruption of the permanent successors.[88] **(Refer Chapter 17, Fig.14: Removable acrylic partial denture).**

2.<u>Removable Distal shoe maintainer</u>

If one or both second primary molars are lost at a short time before the eruption of the first permanent molars, the acrylic removable appliance can be considered in preference to one of the distal shoe maintainers described previously.[88]

An immediate acrylic partial denture with an acrylic distal shoe extension has been used successfully to guide first permanent molar into position. The tooth to be extracted is cut away from the stone model to allow the fabrication of the acrylic extension. The acrylic will extend into the alveolus after the removal of the primary tooth. The extension may be removed after the eruption of the permanent tooth. The contraindications for this appliance are same as previously discussed with the fixed distal shoe appliance.

3.<u>Full or complete dentures</u>

Sometimes all the primary teeth of a preschool child may be recommended for extractions. Although this procedure was more common in prefluoridation era, even today some of the children must have all their teeth removed due to rampant caries and because the teeth are unrestorable. The school age children can wear complete dentures successfully before the eruption of permanent teeth.

The construction of the dentures will result in an improved appearance and the restored function and may be effective in guiding the first permanent molars into their correct position to some extent.[88]**(Refer Chapter 17, Fig.9: Complete acrylic denture).**

14. Space Regainers

Space maintenance is necessary in early loss of posterior primary teeth because early loss contributes to the development of occlusal disharmonies. However, when space is progressively lost, as we have discussed in space closures following early loss of primary teeth, the therapy should be considered to regain it so that additional disharmonies do not develop. Then the regained space is maintained. [92]

CLASSIFICATION

1. Fixed:

    a. Open coil

    b. Gerber

    c. Hotz

    d. Sectional

    e. Lip bumper

2. Removable:

    a. Free end loop

    b. Split saddle

    c. Jack screw

    d. Sling shot

Diagnosis

Accurate diagnosis is crucial for space regaining or any tooth movement. Focusing solely on the segment with the missing tooth often leads to failure. Treatment planning should consider the alignment and space requirements of the entire arch, the relationship of teeth to the denture bases and cranium, and the soft tissue profile.

The diagnostic aids necessary to develop a database for the above consideration include study models, radiographs of all the periapical structures, clinical assessment of facial symmetry and proportions, and possibly cephalometric analysis.

Clinically we have to make quick assessment to determine unfavorable skeletal patterns or dental malocclusions. When the clinical assessment has ruled out the presence of a dental or skeletal class II, class III, open bite or closed bite relationship, there may still exist variations in the class 1 malocclusion in which simple measures at regaining space should not be the only consideration. Assessment of soft tissue profile will help to identify cases in which relative protrusion or retrusion of the dental alveolar structures does complicate evaluation of available space. Correction of protrusion or retrusion will require more than simple regaining of space.

Radiographs and study models will aid significantly in assessing space needs and consideration of tooth alignment. It is important to recognize whether teeth have moved bodily into the space or have tipped axially, because forces applied to tip teeth back into a proper alignment are easier to manage than forces required to bodily return teeth to their proper position in the arch. Another component of database requires visualizing the proximity of adjacent erupting teeth [especially second molars] and estimating their potential impact on the teeth that have crowded the space. Radiographs of the periapical structures are necessary.[92]

Several problems are associated with the regaining procedures. Usually, minimal space loss can be regained better. The space regaining procedure that involves tipping of first permanent molar can be accomplished more easily in the maxillary arch than in the mandibular arch. The procedure should be limited to those cases in which the occlusion is class I, there is adequate anchorage, the second permanent molar is unerupted, and there is a favorable relationship of the second permanent molar with the first permanent molar.

When appliances are used to reposition first permanent molars, there will be reciprocal force exerted to the teeth and supporting tissues anterior to the space, and the result may be undesirable flaring of the anterior teeth. This particularly occurs during the mixed dentition period when the permanent incisors are incompletely erupted and adversely influenced by even minimal forces.

Furthermore, the forward movement of the unerupted second permanent molar accompanies the forward movement of the first molar, and any attempt to tip or reposition the first permanent molar may produce an impaction of the second molar.

If the favorable conditions exist, an attempt to regain space is certainly indicated. Several fixed and removable appliances for space regaining procedures were evolved i.e., tipping of the first molars. However, the distal movement other than minimal tipping can most satisfactorily achieved by Head gear appliance.[92]

FIXED SPACE REGAINERS

CONSTRUCTION OF A SIMPLE APPLIANCE TO REPOSITION THE DISTALLY POSITIONED BICUSPID

FRED EHRLICH [1958] stated that if the first premolar has already erupted and drifted distally, a reciprocal active fixed regainer can be used to good advantage in the mandibular arch. A molar band is fitted to the first permanent molar. Molar tubes are soldered or spot welded in a horizontal position both buccally and lingually to the band. Impressions will be taken with alginate. The tubes will furnish enough of the undercut to lock the band into the impression material while vibrating the stone mix. Make sure to put some wax in the tubes before seating the band in the impression.

A stainless-steel wire which is slightly smaller than the tube size is selected and bent in a U shape. The base of the U should contain a reverse bend to contact the distal surface of the first premolar. As the wire comes out of the tube it should aim toward the first premolar at a point just below the greatest distal convexity of the first premolar. A stop should be placed on both arms where the straight part meets the bend of the wire.

A spaced coil spring is selected which will slide on the wire and is cut about 2 to 3 mm longer than the distance from the anterior stop to the molar tube. When all these parts are ready the band is removed from the working model by heating the stone molar and plunging it into water. The friable stone residue can easily be removed by scraping and cutting with a laboratory knife. Then the parts are cleaned, assembled and the band is cemented with coil springs compressed between the stop and molar tube once in place, the reciprocal action of the coil spring will upright the premolar readily and the molar somewhat. If the diagnosis is correct and the treatment plan has been carried out quickly enough, room for the second premolar is regained, provided there really was room for it.[24]

JAFFE APPLIANCE

An appliance for certain minor tooth movements was described by **PAUL E. JAFFE [1963],** is useful when the presence of the ankylosed tooth, early loss of a deciduous molar or an extraction result in filling of adjacent segments into proximal dental area. Movement is obtained by the use of light spring pressure against a sliding section or arch. The appliance consists of buccal and lingual arms with the sliding arch section. Springs are used in between soldered part of the buccal and lingual arms of the molar bands and the sliding arch to move the desired tooth or teeth.[94]

<u>GERBER SPACE MAINTAINER</u>

This type of appliance may be fabricated directly in the mouth during one relatively short appointment and requires no lab work. A seamless orthodontic band or crown is selected for the abutment tooth and fitted, and the mesial surface is marked for placement of 'U' assembly, which may be welded or soldered in place with silver solder and fluoride flux. The wire U section is fitted in the tube, the appliance placed and wire section extended to contact the tooth mesial to the edentulous area. **(Refer Chapter 17, Fig.15: Gerber space regainer).**

A marking file or pencil is used to establish proper position. Assembly is removed and welded or soldered at this point [upper right]. Expanded center and lower left views show occlusal rest added to wire section to reduce cantilever effect. If appliance is to be used as a spring – loaded space regainer, tube and wire 'U' assembly are not welded. An eyelet may be welded to a flattened part of the tube next to the band, weldable tube stops are soldered on wire portion and open coil spring sections are cut to fit over wire between 'stops' and ends of U – tube. The length of the push coil springs is established by placing the band- tube-wire assembly in the mouth, extending the wire to the desired length, in contact with the mesial tooth and measuring the distance between the tube stops on the wire and the end of the "U" tube. To this distance, add the amount of space needed in the regainer, plus 1 to 2 mm, to ensure spring activation and cut springs to this length. Load springs, tie floss or steel ligature through eyelet and over "U" wire to hold stored force in compressed springs enough to allow the assembly to fit the edentulous area. After cementation, cut the ligature and remove the activate regainer.[98]

HOTZ LINGUAL ARCH

Another method for moving molar distally utilizes the looped Hotz lingual [**HITCHCOCK 1974**]. This is appropriate in a situation where the lower first permanent molar has drifted mesially, but the premolar or cuspid has not drifted distally.

But there must be x-ray evidence that there is sufficient space between first molar and developing second molar. The lingual arch provides compound anchorage from all the other teeth which the lingual arch touches. A horizontal spur can be soldered perpendicular to the arch wire contacting the distal surface of the premolar canine. **(Refer Chapter 17, Fig.16: Hotz lingual arch).**

This compounds the anchorage additionally. The loop on the active side is adjusted periodically [once a month]. After adjustment, the post in the passive position should be approximately 1 mm distal to their tubes. The arch is then forced forward and the posts slipped down into place.[8]

KING APPLIANCE

KING – [1977] described an appliance for regaining of space in both maxillary and mandibular arch. The anchorage unit for the mandibular arch is basically a fixed lingual arch with bands fitted on the first deciduous molar of the treatment side and the first permanent molar on the opposite side. Then a wide siamose edgewise bracket is spot welded to the buccal surface of the primary molar band, and the completed anchorage unit is cemented in place. A band with an angulated buccal tube is cemented on the malpositioned molar, and a straight section of wire with an open coil spring is introduced into the buccal tube and ligated into the bracket.

The anchorage unit must be modified for treatment in the maxillary arch. A millimeter a month is satisfactory progress in the repositioning of first molar. When a class 1 or cusp to cusp molar relation is achieved, a conventional space maintaining appliance should be given. [99]

A SECTIONAL ARCH TECHNIQUE TO REGAIN SPACE

TINGINYS [1978] presented a sectional arch technique to regain lost arch length. Upto 4 millimeters of space can be regained in an effective and efficient manner by the method described It can be used in the cases where the second molar is erupted.[78]

Direct technique:

The cuspid, bicuspid and first molar teeth are banded with edgewise buccal brackets and lingual buttons. The edgewise brackets should have the necessary torque built in as this simplifies treatment. The first sectional arch wire is 0.016-inch diameter and should formed as shown in diagram. After two months a 0.020 arch wire is inserted with the same design as the 0.016. After three or four months, 0.025 x 0.018 rectangular sectional arch is placed. This is the final arch wire and acts as a retainer while waiting for the premolar to erupt, which may take as long as six to eight months. Only a large loop is necessary in this wire.[100]

When the arch wire is tied in place with the ligature wire, the force will be to tip the molar distally and intrude the cuspid and first bicuspid. The location of the second molar is important. If it is unerupted, then tipping the first molar distal may impact it. Radiograph should be taken to fore see this potential problem.

The presence of an erupted second molar is not a contraindication to treatment. A spring separator can be inserted between the first and second molars, as this prevents friction and binding and facilitates tooth movement.

The arch wire should follow the contour of the dental arch in order to prevent buccal movement of the cuspid and first bicuspid. The lingual buttons on the cuspid and premolar should be tied together with 0. 010 ligature wire to provide more stability to the anchor teeth. Adjustments at the circle of the arch are made at monthly intervals. If the second premolar erupts rotated, it must be banded by using lingual buttons, buccal brackets and elastic ligatures so that it can be correctly aligned.[78]

Indirect technique

The teeth are separated and an alginate impression taken. An orthodontic laboratory can adapt bands with torqued edgewise brackets and lingual buttons on the study model.

Other types of fixed space regainers will include head gear appliance used for maxilla, lip bumper used for mandible. These are the interceptive appliances which are used when second permanent molar is already erupted into the oral cavity. These were not discussed in this topic.[78]

ANTERIOR SPACE REGAINER

BAYARDO [1986] described an anterior space regainer utilizing direct bonding technique.

A four-year-old boy presented, with a maxillary primary right central incisor missing, extracted four months earlier. The space was partially lost and the anterior teeth has drifted to the space.

After prophylaxis two 0.018 x 0.025 standard labial tubes were adapted into the mouth. A stainless-steel mesh was spot welded and trimmed to the tubes.

The enamel of the labial surfaces of left central and right lateral incisors was etched with 35% phosphoric acid and each labial tube was individually bonded to each abutment tooth. When the composite polymerized, a piece of 0.014 standard round wire was introduced into the lateral incisor tube.

The wire was then inserted in a 0.036 x 0.009 open coil spring previously selected and passed through the labial tube of the central incisor. A distal bend was made 2 mm from the distal ends of the tubes.

After three weeks, the coil spring was activated and after the space was slightly over widened, a 0.016 round wire was inserted with the same coil spring. Three weeks later the wire was changed to a 0.018 and finally to a 0.018 x 0.025 wire, leaving the coil spring only for retention.

Five weeks later, an acrylic pontic was fixed over the wire and coil spring, using the same type of composite already in the patient's mouth.

<u>LIP BUMPER</u>

Most easily used for space regaining procedure in which bilateral movement is desired. It consists of a heavy labial arch wire over which an acrylic flange is prepared in the anterior region such that it does not contact the lower anterior teeth. It is used to relieve the lip pressure. **(Refer Chapter 17, Fig.9: Lip bumper).**

This pressure can be used to distalized the molars by:

1. Incorporating loops in the arch wire just before it enters the buccal tube.

2. Utilizing a coil spring.

It can also be used unilaterally.[65]

<u>REMOVABLE SPACE REGAINERS</u>

WILLIAM G. GOODALE - [1957] described three types of removable space regainers

<u>FREE END LOOP SPRING SPACE REGAINER</u>

It utilizes a labial arch wire for stability and retention, with a back-action loop action loop spring constructed of no. 0.025 wire. The base of the appliance is made of acrylic resin. Movement of the permanent molar is achieved by activating the free end of the wire loop at certain intervals of time. A light force on the tooth to be moved is desired. The appliance should be checked and adjusted as often as necessary to maintain the light force on the molar. The type of loop spring wire can be changed to fit any situation, depending on the position of the tooth and the distance it needs to be moved.

A free- end loop space regainer for the lower arch has a shorter wire loop, resulting in less distortion when the child inserts the appliance. [82]

<u>SPLIT – BLOCK SPACE REGAINER</u>

It is also called split saddle space regainer. It differs from the free end spring type in that the functional part of the appliance consists of an acrylic block that is split buccolingually and joined by no.0.025 wire in the form of a buccal and a lingual loop. The appliance is activated by periodic spreading of the loops. The activator block is split with a disk after the appliance has been processed. The activator portion of the slit block appliance is essentially the same as one that has been designed to establish space for fixed bridge therapy. The unilateral type used for adults should not be used in the child's mouth, however because of the risks of loss or swallowing. [82]

FIXED, LOOP – SPRING SPACE REGAINERS

It differs from other types only in the design of the spring activation. This appliance resists breakage and provides a satisfactory method of moving the molar distally. The mesial portion of the spring loop is embedded in the resin and passed out through the edentulous space. This portion of wire should contact the distal surface of the tooth which is mesial to the space. This prevents distal movement of this tooth.

A loop is then formed and the wire returned back to contact the mesial surface of the first permanent molar. At this end, the wire is bend around a staple embedded in the resin. The spring loop should be allowed to move freely on the staple. [101]

Retention of this appliance is gained by the use of wire clasps. Orthodontic wire of no. 0.025 or no. 0.030 dimension is embedded in the acrylic resin, brought through the embrasure and then bend down to contact the teeth below the contact points. After the desired movement of the permanent molar has been attained, the appliance may be used as a space maintainer by soldering the activator portion of the spring to the guide wire in its passive position, or by filling in the edentulous region with additional resin.[82]

SLING SHOT SPACE REGAINER

This consists of a wire elastic holder with hooks instead of wire spring that transmits a force against the molar to be distalized. This is called sling shot appliance, since the distalizing force is produced by the elastic stretched on the middle of the lingual surface of the molar to be moved. The other is arranged in the same position on the buccal surface of the molar. The child places a new elastic between the hooks while the appliance is outside the mouth. It is slipped into place; then the child's fingers can guide the elastic into place snugly against the gingival on the mesial margin of the molar to be distalized. The elastic can be changed once each day.[92]

RECALL AND FOLLOW – UP TREATMENT

As we have discussed earlier space maintenance is a dynamic process and should be evaluated continuously. We should not take it granted that we have given the appliance and it will take care of everything. Patient should be recalled for every 2 to 3 months for checkup.

If the appliance is of removable type, we should check whether the patient is using it or not, or any distortions or breakage of the appliance or irritation of soft tissue. If the teeth are emerging underneath the appliance the portion of the acrylic is cutoff to give way for the teeth to erupt into position.

In case of fixed appliance, we have to check whether any breakage of the appliance at the soldered joints or band material. And also check the appliance is loose due to dissolution of cement which may result in food lodgment and caries.

The appliance is removed every 6 months or one year depending on the situation and the abutment tooth is checked for any caries or decalcification. Polishing of the abutment is done followed by fluoride application. Then the appliance is recemented in position.

Regular radiographic examination of developing permanent teeth also necessary. The appliance can be removed or discarded soon after the succedaneous teeth erupted into proper position in the oral cavity.[79]

15. Recent Advances

Space maintainers fabricated using CAD-CAM or 3D printing technology, incorporating modern biocompatible materials, are referred to as 'Digital Space Maintainers.' This advanced approach helps address many of the limitations and challenges associated with conventional fabrication methods. [53]

Steps in Fabrication Using CAD/CAM Technology:

With CAD-CAM technology, dental restorations can be virtually designed and precisely milled using automated equipment. Fabrication typically occurs in a dental laboratory, where the process often begins with a conventional impression taken by the dentist and then converted into a digital format. The introduction of chairside CAD-CAM systems—such as the CEREC system by Sirona—has enabled clinicians to design and produce restorations directly within the dental office. This integration of both chairside and lab-based digital workflows has significantly accelerated the restoration process.

The digital workflow for restorations generally involves three main steps:

(1) Digitally scanning the tooth structure to obtain accurate data;

(2) Using specialized software to design a 3D model of the restoration; and

(3) Fabricating the final restoration from this model using advanced production methods.

<u>**Three-dimensional (3D) Print Technology:**</u>

Additive manufacturing, also known as layered manufacturing or solid freeform fabrication, refers to the process commonly called 3D printing. This innovative technique involves using a digital model to build objects layer by layer, allowing the creation of complex shapes and geometries. Each individual layer corresponds to a cross-sectional slice of the final product. Pawar was the first to apply digital 3D printing technology in the fabrication of space maintainers (SMs), utilizing materials such as titanium-based metal powder and clear photopolymer resin. As noted by the author, 3D printing holds promising applications in the field of pediatric dentistry.

<u>**Advantages:**</u>

1. **Esthetic** – Enhances patient satisfaction and acceptance.

2. **Metal-free** – Ideal for patients with metal or nickel allergies, and those requiring frequent MRIs (e.g., for epilepsy or vascular monitoring).

3. **Precise** – Minimizes deformation, errors, breakage, and decementation.

4. **Quick fabrication time** – Fewer dental visits, improving patient compliance.

5. **Single-unit appliance** – Offers high strength, reducing the risk of fracture and failure.

6. **Smooth surface** – Easier to clean and polish, promoting better gingival health.

7. **Lightweight** – Increases overall comfort for the patient.

8. **No band pinching** – Eliminates discomfort associated with traditional band placement.

<u>Disadvantages:</u>

1. Expensive.

2. Lab assistance is required.

3. Fabrication expertise is required.

4. Expensive equipment is required.

16.Conclusion

According to the literature, conventional band and loop methods, utilized for maintaining space have long been hindered by disadvantages such as cement disintegration, inability to prevent rotation or tipping of adjacent teeth, and increased chair side and laboratory time, making the procedure cumbersome.

To overcome these challenges, prefabricated bands in various sizes were introduced though limitations persisted, highlighting the need for newer appliance designs and materials. Glass Fiber-Reinforced Composite Resins (FRCRs) have emerged as an alternative to conventional space maintainers, particularly in the pediatric dental market. Ribbond, a specific FRCR, offers an aesthetically pleasing option for space maintenance, being well-tolerated by patients and requiring less time. However, limited literature is available regarding its efficacy and longevity.

The field of pediatric dentistry is experiencing a shift towards custom orthodontics with the continuous evolution of dentistry's digital workflow. Digital fabrication techniques enable the creation of reliable and long-lasting space maintainers, eliminating time-consuming manual fabrication stages through CAD-CAM technology. As the digital age progresses and offers various advantages, it is likely that more clinicians will incorporate these techniques into their daily practices, opening the door for investigating new materials and developing more sophisticated appliances in the future.

17. Visual Guide

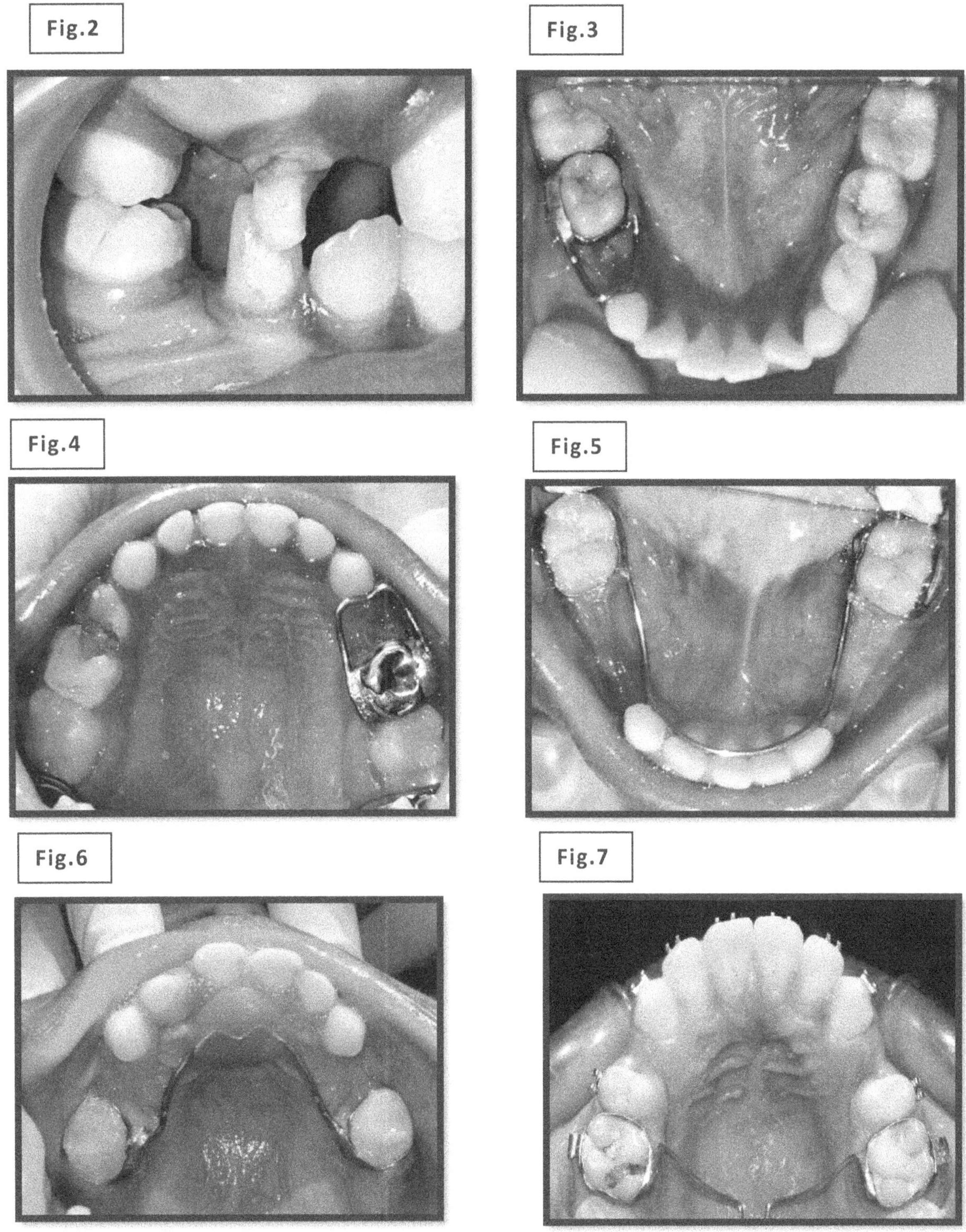

Fig.9

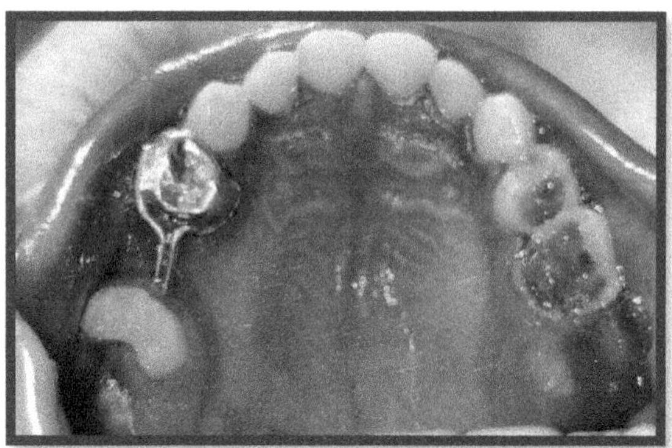

Fig.10

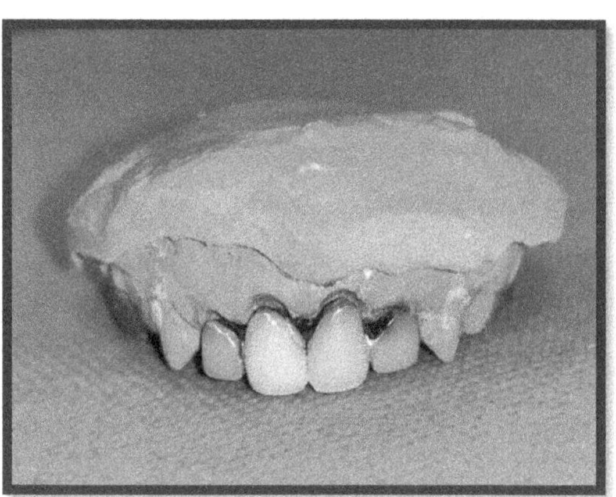
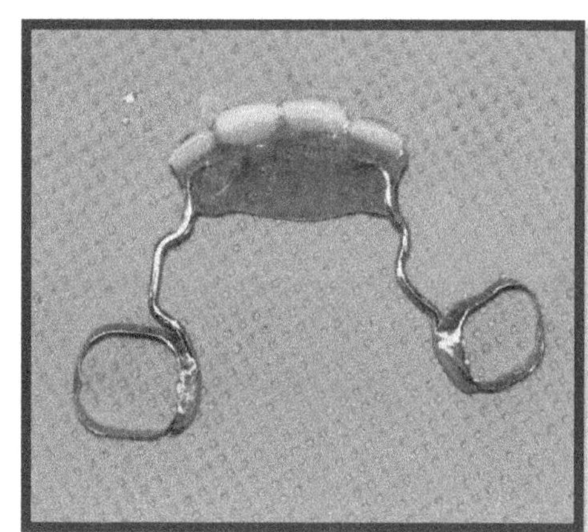

Fig.11

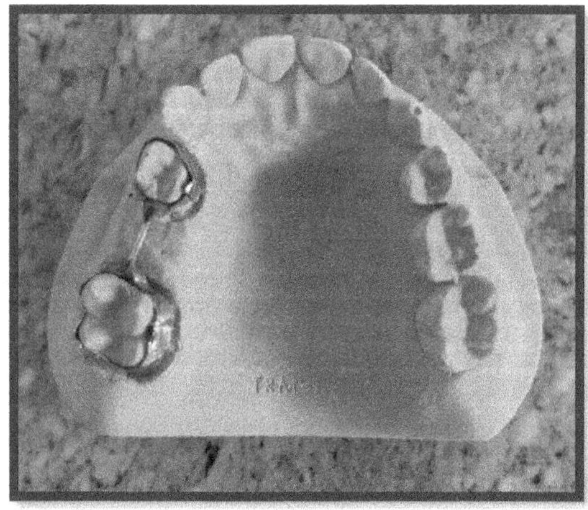

Fig.12

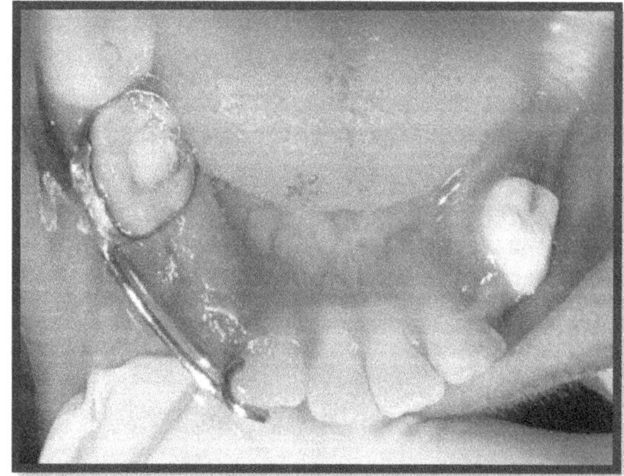

Fig.13

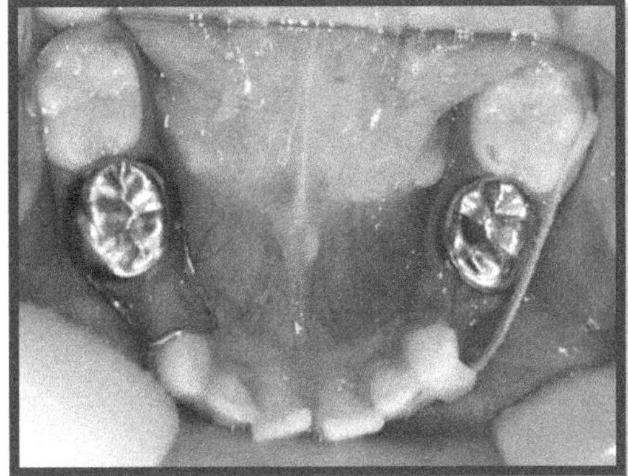

Fig.14

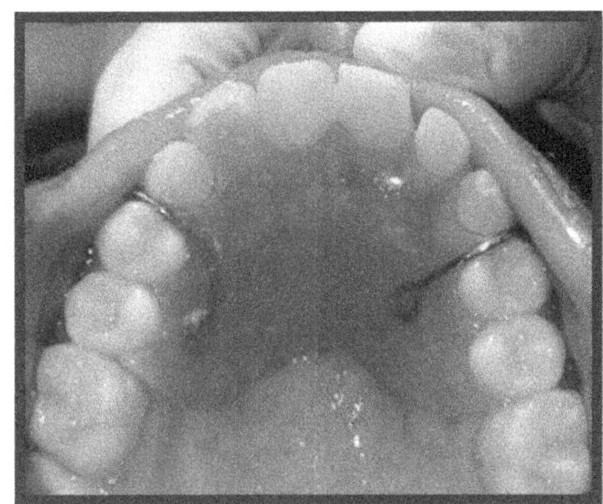

Fig.15

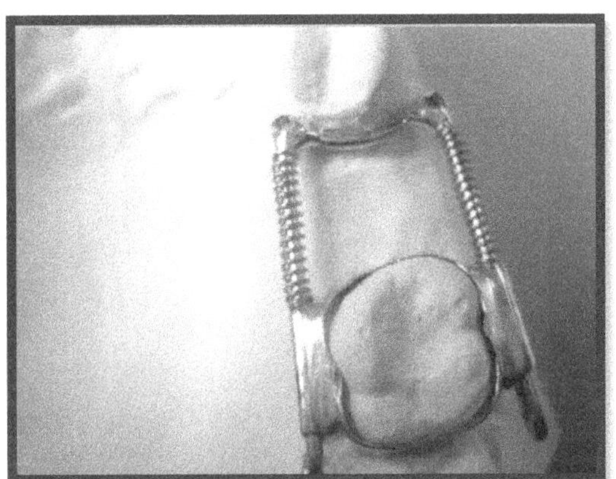

Fig.16

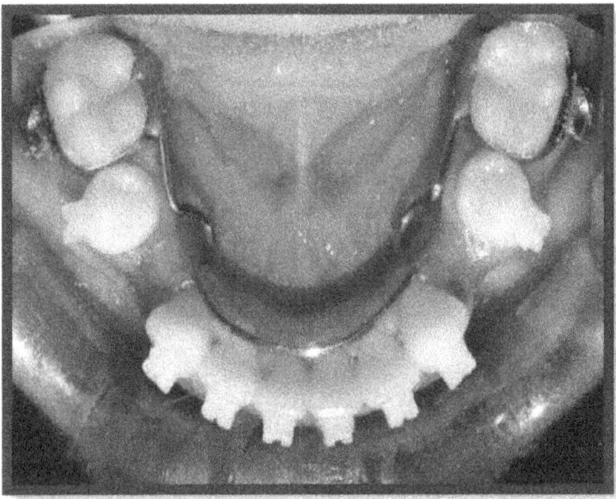

Fig.17

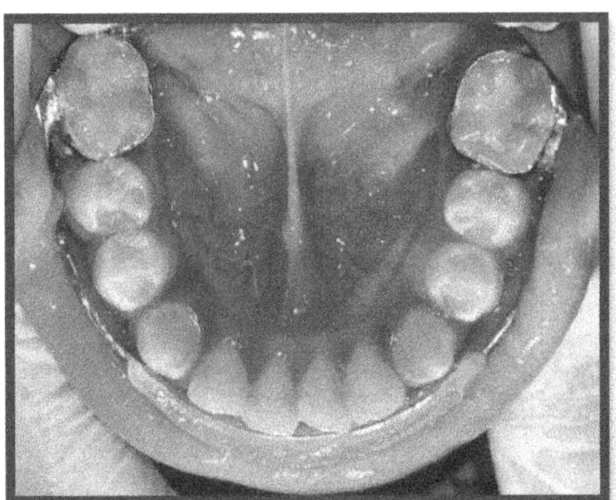

18.References

1. Vittoba Setty J, Srinivasan I. Knowledge and Awareness of Primary Teeth and Their Importance among Parents in Bengaluru City, India. Int J Clin Pediatr Dent. 2016 Jan-Mar;9(1):56-61.

2. FAUCHARD [18th century]. Quoted in Martinez, Norman, p., Elsbac, Henry g.Funtional maintenance of arch-length.J. Dent. Child 51 [3]: 190-193, 1984.

3. HUNTER, J. [1839].Quoted in Martinez, Norman, P., Elsbach, B.SFuntional maintenance of arch-length.J. Dent. Child 51 [3]: 190-193,1984.

4. WALTHER, D.P.Current Orthodontics. Bristol J. Wright, p. 219-222, 1966.

5. SCHWARTZ, DR. ERNEST.Space maintenance, Technique clinic. J. Clinic. Orhodont. 12 [4]: 299, 1978.

6. DAVEY, K.W.Effect of premature loss of primary molars on the anteroposterior position of maxillary permanent molars and other maxillary teeth. J. Dent. Child 34: 383-394, Sept. 1967.

7. MaC LAUGHLIN, J.A., FOGELS, H.R. and SHIERE, F.R. The influence of premature primary molar extraction on bicuspid eruption J. Dent.child 34:399-405,Sept. 1967.

8. HITCHCOCK, H.P.Orthodontics for undergraduates.Lea and Febiger, Philadelphia, p.226-273, 1974.

9. Nagaveni NB, Radhika NB, Umashankar KV. Knowledge, attitude and practices of parents regarding primary teeth care of their children in Davangere city, India. Pesq Bras Odontoped Clin Integr, Joao Pessoa. 2011 Jan;11(1):129–132.

10. Ahuja V, Thosar NR, Shrivastav S, Ahuja A. Effect of Lingual Arch Space Maintainer on the Position of Mandibular Molars and Incisors in the Vertical Direction during the Resolution of Mandibular Incisors Crowding: A Systematic Review . Int J Clin Pediatr Dent. 2021;14.

11. Watt, E., Ahmad, A., Adamji, R. et al. Space maintainers in the primary and mixed dentition – a clinical guide. Br Dent J (2018). 225, 293–298

12. Setia V, Pandit IK, Srivastava N, et al. Space maintainers in dentistry: Pasttopresent.JClinDiagnRes.2013;7(10):24-26

13. Ngan P, Alkire RG, Fields H., Jr Management of space problems in the primary and mixed dentitions. J Am Dent Assoc. 1999;130:1330–9.

14. Durward CS. Space maintenance in the primary and mixed dentition. Ann R Australas Coll Dent Surg. 2000 Oct;15:203-5.

15. Moscovich H, Creugers NHJ. The novel use of extracted teeth as a dental restorative material: the natural inlay. J Dent. 1998. 26:21-24,

16. Cernei ER, Mavru RB, Zetu IN. Axial modifications of permanent lower molars after premature losses of temporary molars. Rev Med Chir Soc Med Nat Iasi. 2016;120:178–85.

17. Macena MC, Tornisiello Katz CR, Heimer MV, de Oliveira e Silva JF, Costa LB. Space changes after premature loss of deciduous molars among Brazilian children. Am J Orthod Dentofacial Orthop. 2011;140:771

18. Cardoso L, Zembruski C, Femandes DS, Boff I, Pessin V. Evaluation of prevalence of malocclusion in relation to premature loss of primary teeth. Pesq Bras Odontoped Clin Integr. 2005;5:17–22.

19. Baratieri LN, Monteiro Jr S, Andrada MAC.The "sandwich" technique as a base for reattachment of dental fragments. Quintessence Int 1991; 22:81-85.

20. Survival of laboratory fabricated space maintainer by Ming Hui Zhao a thesis submitted at by THE UNIVERSITY OF BRITISH COLUMBIA. 2002,30-55

21. WRIGHT, GERALD, Z. and KENNEDY, DAVID, B. Space control in primary and mixed dentition. The Dental clinics of N. America1978. 22[4] : 579-602.

22. PRUHS, RONALD, J. The use of stainless steel crowns in the construction of space maintainers. J. Dent . Child 1978. 45: 293- 295.

23. GAINSFORTH Quoted in Brauer, J.C., Demerit, W.W., Higley, L.B et al Dentistry for children, fourth edition1955. P. 396 -410.

24. BRAUER, J.C., DEMERITT, W.W., HIGLEY, L.B. et al. Dentistry for children, fourth edition. McGraw-Hill Book Company Inc. p.396-435, 1959.

25. Shobhaa Tandon. Pediatric Dentistry 2018 Third edition Pg no:522-534

26. Moyers R E, Riolo M L. Handbook of orthodontics. Chicago, Yearbook medical publishers. Inc., 1988 4th ed. p. 361.

27. MARTINEZ, NORMAN, P., ELSBACH, HENRY,G. Functional maintenance of arch length. J.Dent. child1984.51[3]: 190-193,

28. HILL, C.J., SORENSON, H.W., and MINK, J.R. Space maintenance in a child dental care programme.JADA 1975.90: 811-815,

29. Rapp R, Demiroz I. A new design for space maintainers replacing prematurely lost first primary molars. Pediatr Dent. 1983 Jun;5(2):131-4.

30. Douglass J, Tinanoff N. The etiology, prevalence, and sequelae of infraclusion of primary molars. ASDC J Dent Child. 1991 Nov-Dec;58(6):481-3.

31. Gegenheimer R, Donly KJ. Distal shoe: a cost-effective maintainer for primary second molars. Pediatr Dent. 1992 Jul-Aug;14(4):268-9.

32. Baroni C, Franchini A, Rimondini L. Survival of different types of space maintainers. Pediatr Dent. 1994 Sep-Oct;16(5):360-1.

33. Yonezu T, Machida Y. Occlusal migration of the maxillary first primary molars subsequent to the loss of antagonists. Bull Tokyo Dent Coll. 1997 Aug;38(3):201-6.

34. Qudeimat MA, Fayle SA. The longevity of space maintainers: a retrospective study. Pediatric Dent. 1998;20(4):267-272.

35. Rajab LD. Clinical performance and survival of space maintainers: evaluation over a period of 5 years. ASDC J Dent Child. 2002;69(2):156-124.

36. Kargul B, Caglar E, Kabalay U. Glass fiber reinforced composite resin space maintainer: case reports. J Dent Child (Chic). 2003 Sep-Dec;70(3):258-61.

37. Simsek S, Yilmaz Y, Gurbuz T. Clinical evaluation of simple fixed space maintainers bonded with flow composite resin. J Dent Child (Chic). 2004 May-Aug;71(2):163-8.

38. Kargul B, Caglar E, Kabalay U. Glass fiber-reinforced composite resin as fixed space maintainers in children: 12-month clinical follow-up. J Dent Child (Chic). 2005 Sep-Dec;72(3):109-12.

39. Subramaniam P, Babu G, Sunny R. Glass fiber-reinforced composite resin as a space maintainer: a clinical study. J Indian Soc Pedod Prev Dent. 2008;26 Suppl 3:S98-103.

40. Sasa IS, Hasan AA, Qudeimat MA. Longevity of band and loop space maintainers using glass ionomer cement: a prospective study. Eur Arch Paediatr Dent. 2009 Jan;10(1):6-10.

41. Tunc ES, Bayrak S, Tuloglu N, Egilmez T, Isci D. Evaluation of survival of 3 different fixed space maintainers. Pediatr Dent. 2012 Jul-Aug;34(4):e97-102.

42. Saravanakumar MS, Siddaramayya J, Sajjanar AB, Godhi BS, Reddy NS, Krishnam RP. Fiber technology in space maintainer: a clinical follow-up study. J Contemp Dent Pract. 2013 Nov 1;14(6):1070-5.

43. Qudeimat MA, Sasa IS. Clinical success and longevity of band and loop compared to crown and loop space maintainers. Eur Arch Paediatr Dent. 2015 Oct;16(5):391-6.

44. Kirzioğlu Z, Çiftçi ZZ, Yetiş CÇ. Clinical Success of Fiber-reinforced Composite Resin as a Space Maintainer. J Contemp Dent Pract. 2017 Mar 1;18(3):188-193.

45. Soni HK. Application of CAD-CAM for Fabrication of Metal-Free Band and Loop Space Maintainer. J Clin Diagn Res. 2017 Feb;11(2):ZD14-ZD16.

46. Potgieter N, Brandt PD, Mohamed N. Clinical evaluation of the loop-design fibre-reinforced composite and the band-and-loop space maintainers. J Dent Assoc South Africa 2018 Aug 1;73:436–41.

47. Mittal S, Sharma A, Sharma AK, et al. Banded versus single-sided bonded space maintainers: A comparative study. Indian J Dent Sci. 2018;10(1):29.

48. Yilmaz H, Aydin MN. YouTubeTM video content analysis on space maintainers. J Indian Soc Pedod Prev Dent. 2020 Jan-Mar;38(1):34-40.

49. Rani R, Chachra S, Dhindsa A, Sharma M. Clinical success of fixed space maintainers: Conventional band and loop versus fiber-reinforced composite loop space maintainer. New Niger J Clin Res. 2020 Jan 34(1):35-38.

50. Khanna S, Rao D, Panwar S, Pawar B, Ameen S. 3D Printed Band and Loop Space Maintainer: A Digital Game Changer in Preventive Orthodontics. J Clin Pediatr Dent. 2021 Jul 1;45:147–51.

51. Tyagi M, Rana V, Srivastava N, Kaushik N, Moirangthem E, Gaur V. Comparison of the Conventional Band and Loop Space Maintainers with Modified Space Maintainers: A Split-mouth Randomized Clinical Trial. Int J Clin Pediatr Dent. 2021;14(Suppl 1):S63-S68.

52. Volpato LE, Crivelli AS, Oliveira ET, Nobreza AM, Rosa A. Rehabilitation with Esthetic Functional Fixed Space Maintainer: A Report of Two Cases. Int J Clin Pediatr Dent. 2021 Mar-Apr;14(2):315-318.

53. Dhanotra KG, Bhatia R. Digitainers-Digital Space Maintainers: A Review. Int J Clin Pediatr Dent. 2021;14(Suppl 1):S69-S75.

54. Conventional and CAD/CAM-fabricated band-loop space maintainers. Int J Pediatric Dent. 2022 Sep;32(5):764–71.

55. Watson L, Danley B, Versluis A, Tantbirojn D, Brooks J, Wells MH. A Structural Analysis of 3D Printed Pediatric Space Maintainers. Pediatr Dent. 2023 Jul 15;45(4):342-347.

56. Fathima A, Jeevanandan G. Interrelationship Between Intelligence Quotient and Space Maintainers Among Children: A Cross-Sectional Comparative Study. Cureus.2023;15(12):e50752.

57. Cengiz A, Karayilmaz H. Comparative evaluation of the clinical success of 3D-printed space maintainers and band-loop space maintainers. Int J Paediatr Dent. 2024 Jan 12.242-247

58. THUROW, RAYMOND,C.Atlas of orthodontic principles. C.V. Mosby company, p. 194-197, 1970 Second edition.

59. HINRICHSEN, C.F.L Space maintenance in pedodontics.   Australian D.J. 7: 451-456,1961In year book of dentistry, p. 169-173, 1963-64.

60. JON, T. KAPALA.In Braham, Raymond, l. and Morris, Merle E. edited 1985 Text book of pediatric dentistry, second edition. Williams and wilkins p.610-653,.

61. Merle E.Morris RLB. Textbook of Pediatric Dentistry. Williams and wilkins p.710-735,Second edition 1985.

62. GOULD D. GSpace maintenance. Brit. Dent. J1965..118: 20-26.

63. ENGH, O. BRUK Space maintainers- When and How.Norske Tanbegeforen Tid. 80: 81-90.1970 In Dental abstracts, p. 625-626,.

64. RYAN, KEITH, Understanding and use of space maintenance procedures.J. Dent. Child. 31: 21-25,1964. In year book of dentistry, p.184, 1964-65.

65. N SIVAKUMAR MSM. Pediatric Dentistry Principles and Practice. THIRD edition 2022 Pg no:614-622.

66. Proffit W R, Fields H W, Sarver D M. Contemporary Orthodontics. 4th edition. St Louis: Mosby, 2006 Pg no:533-548.

67. J. Precision lingual arches. Active applic tions. J Clin Orthod 1989; 23: 101–109.

68. Letti HC, Rizzatto SM, de Menezes LM, Reale CS, de Lima EM, Martinelli FL. Sagittal changes in lower incisors by the use of lingual arch. Dental Press J Orthod. 2013;18(3):29-34.

69. Yin Y T J, Lin Y T. Long-term space changes after pre mature loss of a primary maxillary first molar. J Dent Sci 2017; 12: 44–48.

70. Foley, T F, Wright G Z, Weinberger S J. Management of lower incisor crowding in the early mixed dentition. ASDC J Dent Child 1996; 63: 169–174.

71. Fricker J, Kharbanda O P, Dando J. Orthodontic diagnosis and treatment in the mixed dentition. In A Cameron and R Widmer (editors) A Handbook of Paediatric Dentistry. 2013. 3rd ed. London: Mosby Elsevier;

72. Guideline on Management of the Developing Dentition and Occlusion in Pediatric Dentistry. Paediatr Dent 2016; 38: 289–301.

73. TSAMTSOURIS, A., GEORGE, E. WHITE.Space maintainers for the integrity of arch perimeter : Part 1 The Transpalatal arch appliance.J . Pedodontics 1977. 1 [2]: 91-98,

74. GRABER, T.M.Orthodontics principles and practice.Third edition. W.B. Saunders company, 1972. p. 638-660,

75. LEIVESLEY, W.D. Guiding the developing mixed dentition. Australian D.J. 1984. 29[3]: 157.

76. LOUIS, A.N., NANN, A., WICKWIRE and MILTON, E.G.Space management in mixed dentition. J. Dent. Child, 1975. 42:112-18,

77. LOOS, P.L.and CORPRON, R.E. The band and loop space maintainer. J. Michigan Dent. Assn. 54: 365-368, 1972. In dental abstracts p. 306-307,1973.

78. SIMONSEN, R.J. Clinical application of the acid etch technique. Quintessence publishing Co. Inc. p. 1978 113-121,.

79. CHEUNG, W.S. Making band space maintainers.J. Canad. Dent. Assn. 1979 45 [67]: 285-286,.

80. CHAWLA, H.S., GOYAL, A., KHERA, N. Modified space maintainers. J.Ind.Soc. Pedo. Prev. Dent. 19842[1]. 34-35 ,.

81. ROBERTS, MICHAEL, W. An esthetic self-adjusting appliance for primary anterior space maintenance.In dental abstracts, p. 200, 1972. J. New jersey Dent. Assn. 1971. 44: 6-7,

82. GOODALE, WILLIAM, G Restoration of space for second bicuspid eruption. In Dental abstracts Volume 2 1958., p. 205,

83. HICKS, E. PRESTON.Treatment planning for the distal shoe space maintainer.The Dental clinics of N. America1973. 17[1]: 135-149,

84. BARBER, THOMAS, KSpace management .In Barber, T.K. and Luke, L.S.edited.Pediatric dentistry.John Wright PSB Inc. 1982. p.223-246,

85. LEVITL,B Loss of deciduous molar prior to eruption of the first permanent mola J.clin.Orthodont. 1971. 510- 512

86. BEAVER, HARVEY,A., and KOPEL,A. A New appliance for space maintenanJ. Michigan. Dent. Assn. 49:299-300, 1967.In Dental Abstracts,p.99-100,

87. HUNTER, SHERYL, B.Space maintenance with the Garcia-godoy appliance. J. Clin. Orthodont. 23[8]; 529-531,1989.

88. Mc DONALD, R.E.and AVERY, D.R. Dentistry for the child and adolescent, Eleventh edition 2022, The C.V. Mosby company.Pg no: 255-268.

89. SCHACHTER Adjustable space maintainer for general practitionerJADA66: 817-820,1963.In year book of dentistry , p.191, 1963-64.

90. SWAINE, T. J. and WRIGHT, G.ZDirect bonding applied to the space maintenance. J . Dent.child1976. 43[6] : 401-405,

91. WILSON, WILLIAM , L., WILSON, ROBERT, C.3D instant space maintainer.J. Clin. Orthodont. 1984. 18 [8]: 892-893,

92. SIM, JOSEPH. M Minor tooth movement in children, 2nd edition. C. V. Mosby company, 1977.987-990.

93. CROLL, THEODORE, P.Cementation of stainless steel space maintainers J. Pedodontics 7[2]: 1983 120-126,.

94. JAFFE, PAUL,E.Appliance for certain minor tooth movement.New York D.J. 1963. 29: 78-85,

95. ARTUM, J., MARSTRANDER, P.BClinical efficiency of two different types of direct bonded space maintainers. J.Dent.Child 50: 197 -204,1983.

96. ATHANASIOS, A., NICOLAS, F. New Universal Space maintainer. J. Clinical. Orthodont. 1984. 18 [8]: 570 -571,

97. RUBEN, E. BAYARDO. Anterior space maintainer and regainer.J. Dent .Child (1986) 53.: 452-455,

98. SIMON, JOHN, F. JR., FARRAGE, JAMES, R. and MISNER, L.R. JR. Regaining space in the mixed dentition.The dental clinics of north America 22[4] 1978. : 669-684.

99. KING, DAVID, L.A space regaining procedure for the early mixed dentition. Gen.Dent. 24: 44-45, 1976. In dental abstracts p.293-295.

100. Wright GZ, Kennedy DB. Space control in the primary and mixed dentitions. Dent Clin   North Am. 1978 Oct;22(4):579-601.

101. Karaman AI, Kir N, Belli S. Four applications of reinforced polyethylene fiber material in orthodontic practice. Am J Orthod Dentofacial Orthop. 2002 Jun;121(6):650-4.

102. Ricketts RM. Bioprogressive therapy as an answer to orthodontic needs. Part I. Am J Orthod. 1976 Sep;70(3):241-68.